Internet of Things Programming with JavaScript

Learn the art of bringing the Internet of Things into your projects with the power of JavaScript

Rubén Oliva Ramos

BIRMINGHAM - MUMBAI

Internet of Things Programming with JavaScript

First published: February 2017

Production reference: 1150217

Published by Packt Publishing Ltd.
Livery Place
35 Livery Street
Birmingham
B3 2PB, UK.
ISBN 978-1-78588-856-4

www.packtpub.com

Credits

Author

Rubén Oliva Ramos

Reviewer

Jacqueline Wilson

Commissioning Editor

Wilson D'souza

Acquisition Editor

Tushar Gupta

Content Development Editor

Aishwarya Pandere

Technical Editor

Karan Thakkar

Copy Editor

Safis Editing

Project Coordinator

Nidhi Joshi

Proofreader

Safis Editing

Indexer

Pratik Shirodkar

Production Coordinator

Nilesh Mohite

About the Author

Rubén Oliva Ramos is a computer systems engineer, with a master's degree in computer and electronic systems engineering, teleinformatics and networking specialization from University of Salle Bajio in Leon, Guanajuato Mexico. He has more than five years of experience in: developing web applications to control and monitor devices connected with Arduino and Raspberry Pi using web frameworks and cloud services to build Internet of Things applications.

He is a mechatronics teacher at University of Salle Bajio and teaches students on the master's degree in Design and Engineering of Mechatronics Systems. He also works at Centro de Bachillerato Tecnologico Industrial 225 in Leon, Guanajuato Mexico, teaching the following: electronics, robotics and control, automation, and microcontrollers at Mechatronics Technician Career. He has worked on consultant and developer projects in areas such as monitoring systems and datalogger data using technologies such as Android, iOS, Windows Phone, Visual Studio .NET, HTML5, PHP, CSS, Ajax, JavaScript, Angular, ASP .NET databases (SQlite, mongoDB, and MySQL), and web servers (Node.js and IIS). Ruben has done hardware programming on Arduino, Raspberry Pi, Ethernet Shield, GPS and GSM/GPRS, ESP8266, and control and monitor systems for data acquisition and programming.

"I want to thank God for helping me writing this book and his inspiration, to my wife, Mayte, and my sons, Ruben and Dario, for their support while writing this book and in general for their support in all my projects. To my parents, my brother and sister whom I love.

I hope this book covers the main topics for students that want to learn more about Internet of Things projects, and all the prerequisites for building this kind of application."

www.packtpub.com

For support files and downloads related to your book, please visit www.PacktPub.com.

Did you know that Packt offers eBook versions of every book published, with PDF and ePub files available? You can upgrade to the eBook version at www.PacktPub.com and as a print book customer, you are entitled to a discount on the eBook copy. Get in touch with us at service@packtpub.com for more details.

At www.PacktPub.com, you can also read a collection of free technical articles, sign up for a range of free newsletters and receive exclusive discounts and offers on Packt books and eBooks.

https://www.packtpub.com/mapt

Get the most in-demand software skills with Mapt. Mapt gives you full access to all Packt books and video courses, as well as industry-leading tools to help you plan your personal development and advance your career.

Why subscribe?

- Fully searchable across every book published by Packt
- Copy and paste, print, and bookmark content
- On demand and accessible via a web browser

Customer Feedback

Thanks for purchasing this Packt book. At Packt, quality is at the heart of our editorial process. To help us improve, please leave us an honest review on this book's Amazon page at `https://goo.gl/pZ7EFn`.

If you'd like to join our team of regular reviewers, you can e-mail us at `customerreviews@packtpub.com`. We award our regular reviewers with free eBooks and videos in exchange for their valuable feedback. Help us be relentless in improving our products!

Table of Contents

Preface

The Raspberry Pi Zero is a powerful, low-cost, credit-card sized computer, which lends itself perfectly to begin the controller of sophisticated home automation devices. Using the available on-board interfaces, the Raspberry Pi Zero can be expanded to allow the connection of a virtually infinite number of security sensors and devices.

Since the Arduino platform is more versatile and useful for making projects, including the networking applications of the Internet of Things, this is what we will see in this book: the integration of devices connected to the nodes using the amazing and important Arduino board, and how to integrate the Raspberry Pi Zero to control and monitor the devices from a central interface working as a hub. With software programming you will create an Internet of Things system based in developing technologies such as JavaScript, HTML5, and Node.js.

This is exactly what I will teach you to do in this book. You will learn how to use the Raspberry Pi Zero board in several home domotics projects in order for you to build your own.

The books guides you, making the projects in each chapter from preparing the field, the hardware, the sensors, the communication, and the software programming-control in order to have a complete control and monitoring system.

What this book covers

Chapter 1, *Getting Started with Raspberry Pi Zero*, describes the procedure to set up the Raspberry Pi and the Arduino board, and how to communicate among the devices. We will install and set up the operating system, connect our Pi to the network, and access it remotely. We'll also secure our Pi and make sure it can keep the right time.

Chapter 2, *Connecting Things to the Raspberry Pi Zero*, shows how to connect signals to the Raspberry Pi Zero and Arduino. It explores the GPIO port and the various interfaces it features. We'll look at the various things we can connect to the Raspberry Pi using the GPIO.

Chapter 3, *Connecting sensors - Measure the Real Things*, shows how to implement the sensors for detecting different kinds of signal, for security systems, flow current for energy consumption, detecting some risk in the home, implementing a gas sensor, flow water sensor to measure water volume, and will also show how to make a security system that will control entrance to the home with a fingerprint sensor.

Chapter 4, *Control-connected devices*, shows how to control your Arduino board, using modules of communication in a networking area from the Raspberry Pi Zero in a central interface dashboard.

Chapter 5, *Adding a Webcam to Monitor Your Security System*, shows how to configure a webcam connected to your board to monitor your security system for the Internet of Things.

Chapter 6, *Building a Web Monitor and Controlling Devices from a Dashboard*, shows how to set up a system to monitor your security system using web services. Integrating the Raspberry Pi Zero with Arduino to build a complete system connected-devices and monitor.

Chapter 7, *Building a Spy Police with the Internet of Things dashboard*, shows how to make different mini home domotics projects and how to connect web services and monitor your security system using the Internet of Things.

Chapter 8, *Monitor and Control your devices from a Smart Phone*, explains how to develop an app for Smart Phone using Android Studio and APP inventor, and control your Arduino board and the Raspberry Pi Zero.

Chapter 9, *Putting It All Together*, shows how to put everything together, all the parts of the project, the electronics field, software configurations, and power supplies.

What you need for this book

You'll need the following software:

- Win32 Disk Imager 0.9.5 PuTTY
- i2C-tools
- WiringPi2 for Python
- Node.js 4.5 or later
- Node.js for Windows V7.3.0 or later
- Python 2.7.x or Python 3.x
- PHP MyAdmin Database

- MySQL module
- Create and account in Gmail so that you can get in APP Inventor
- Android Studio and SDK modules
- Arduino software

In the first chapters, we explain all the basics so you will have everything configured and will be able to use the Raspberry Pi Zero without any problems, so you can use it for the projects in this book. We will use some basic components, such as sensors, and move to more complex components in the rest of the book.

On the software side, it is good if you actually have some existing programming skills, especially in JavaScript and in the Node.js framework. However, I will explain all the parts of each software piece of this book, so even if you don't have good programming skills in JavaScript you will be able to follow along.

Who this book is for

This book is for all the people who want to automate their homes and make them smarter, while at the same time having complete control of what they are doing. If that's your case, you will learn everything there is to learn in this book about how to use the amazing Raspberry Pi Zero board to control your projects.

This book is also for makers who have played in the past with other development boards, such as Arduino. If that's the case, you will learn how to use the power of the Raspberry Pi platform to build smart homes. You will also learn how to create projects that can easily be done with other platforms, such as creating a wireless security camera with the Pi Zero.

Conventions

In this book, you will find a number of text styles that distinguish between different kinds of information. Here are some examples of these styles and an explanation of their meaning.

Code words in text, database table names, folder names, filenames, file extensions, pathnames, dummy URLs, user input, and Twitter handles are shown as follows: "Extract `2015-09-24-raspbian-jessie.img` to your Home folder."

A block of code is set as follows:

```
# passwd
root@raspberrypi:/home/pi# passwd
Enter new UNIX password:
Retype new UNIX password:
passwd: password updated successfully
        root@raspberrypi:/home/pi#
```

When we wish to draw your attention to a particular part of a code block, the relevant lines or items are set in bold:

```
[default]
exten => s,1,Dial(Zap/1|30)
exten => s,2,Voicemail(u100)
exten => s,102,Voicemail(b100)
exten => i,1,Voicemail(s0)
```

Any command-line input or output is written as follows:

```
sudo npm install express request
```

New terms and **important words** are shown in bold. Words that you see on the screen, for example, in menus or dialog boxes, appear in the text like this:

"You can now just click on **Stream** to access the live stream from the camera."

Warnings or important notes appear in a box like this.

Tips and tricks appear like this.

Reader feedback

Feedback from our readers is always welcome. Let us know what you think about this book-what you liked or disliked. Reader feedback is important for us as it helps us develop titles that you will really get the most out of.

To send us general feedback, simply e-mail `feedback@packtpub.com`, and mention the book's title in the subject of your message.

If there is a topic that you have expertise in and you are interested in either writing or contributing to a book, see our author guide at `www.packtpub.com/authors`.

Customer support

Now that you are the proud owner of a Packt book, we have a number of things to help you to get the most from your purchase.

Downloading the example code

You can download the example code files for this book from your account at `http://www.packtpub.com`. If you purchased this book elsewhere, you can visit `http://www.packtpub.com/support` and register to have the files e-mailed directly to you.

You can download the code files by following these steps:

1. Log in or register to our website using your e-mail address and password.
2. Hover the mouse pointer on the **SUPPORT** tab at the top.
3. Click on **Code Downloads & Errata**.
4. Enter the name of the book in the **Search** box.
5. Select the book for which you're looking to download the code files.
6. Choose from the drop-down menu where you purchased this book from.
7. Click on **Code Download**.

Once the file is downloaded, please make sure that you unzip or extract the folder using the latest version of:

- WinRAR / 7-Zip for Windows
- Zipeg / iZip / UnRarX for Mac
- 7-Zip / PeaZip for Linux

The code bundle for the book is also hosted on GitHub at `https://github.com/PacktPublishing/Internet-of-Things-Programming-with-Javascript`. We also have other code bundles from our rich catalog of books and videos available at `https://github.com/PacktPublishing/`. Check them out!

Downloading the color images of this book

We also provide you with a PDF file that has color images of the screenshots/diagrams used in this book. The color images will help you better understand the changes in the output. You can download this file from `https://www.packtpub.com/sites/default/files/down loads/InternetofThingsProgrammingwithJavascript_ColorImages.pdf`.

Errata

Although we have taken every care to ensure the accuracy of our content, mistakes do happen. If you find a mistake in one of our books-maybe a mistake in the text or the code-we would be grateful if you could report this to us. By doing so, you can save other readers from frustration and help us improve subsequent versions of this book. If you find any errata, please report them by visiting `http://www.packtpub.com/submit-errata`, selecting your book, clicking on the **Errata Submission Form** link, and entering the details of your errata. Once your errata are verified, your submission will be accepted and the errata will be uploaded to our website or added to any list of existing errata under the Errata section of that title.

To view the previously submitted errata, go to `https://www.packtpub.com/books/conten t/support` and enter the name of the book in the search field. The required information will appear under the **Errata** section.

Piracy

Piracy of copyrighted material on the Internet is an ongoing problem across all media. At Packt, we take the protection of our copyright and licenses very seriously. If you come across any illegal copies of our works in any form on the Internet, please provide us with the location address or website name immediately so that we can pursue a remedy.

Please contact us at `copyright@packtpub.com` with a link to the suspected pirated material.

We appreciate your help in protecting our authors and our ability to bring you valuable content.

Questions

If you have a problem with any aspect of this book, you can contact us at `questions@packtpub.com`, and we will do our best to address the problem.

1

Getting Started with Raspberry Pi Zero

Before building several projects for a home security system and the control of domestic appliances by electronically controlled systems, in this chapter, we're going to go into an initial configuration and prepare our Raspberry Pi Zero to work in a network, so you can use it for all the projects we will see in this book.

Before we go through the projects, build our network with the devices, and connect our sensor to the boards, it's important to understand the configuration of the Raspberry Pi. The main idea of this chapter is to explain how to set up your Raspberry Pi Zero; we will cover the following topics:

- Setting up Raspberry Pi Zero
- Preparing the SD card
- Installing the Raspbian operating system
- Configuring your Raspberry Pi Zero with a serial console cable
- Accessing the network remotely
- Accessing via remote desktop
- Configuring a web server

Setting up Raspberry Pi Zero

The Raspberry Pi is a low-cost board dedicated to purpose projects. Here, we will use a Raspberry Pi Zero board. Take a look at the following link: `https://www.adafruit.com/products/2816`. I used this board.

In order to make the Raspberry Pi work, we need an operating system that acts as a bridge between the hardware and the user. This book uses the Raspbian Jessy, which can be downloaded from `https://www.raspberrypi.org/downloads/`. At this link, you will find all of the information you need to download all the pieces of software necessary to use with your Raspberry Pi to deploy Raspbian. You need a micro SD card of at least 4 GB.

The kit that I used to test the Raspberry Pi Zero includes all the necessary things for installing everything and getting the board ready:

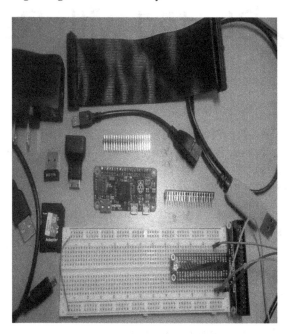

Preparing the SD card

The Raspberry Pi Zero only boots from an SD card and cannot boot from an external drive or USB stick. For this book, it's recommended to use a 4 GB micro SD card.

Installing the Raspbian operating system

There are many operating systems that are available for the Raspberry Pi board, most of which are based on Linux. However, the one that is usually recommended is Raspbian, is an operating system based on Debian, which was specifically made for Raspberry Pi.

In order to install the Raspbian operating system on your Pi, follow the next steps:

1. Download the latest Raspbian image from the official Raspberry Pi website: `http s://www.raspberrypi.org/downloads/raspbian/`

2. Next, insert the micro SD card into your computer using an adapter. (An adapter is usually given with the SD card.)

3. Then download Win32DiskImager from `https://sourceforge.net/projects/w in32diskimager/`.

   You will see the following files, as shown in the screenshot, after downloading the folder:

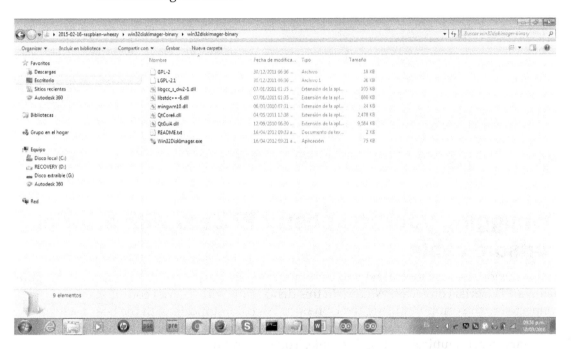

4. Open the file image, select the path where you have the micro SD card, and click on the **Write** button.

5. After a few seconds, you have Raspbian installed on your SD card; insert it into Raspberry Pi and connect the Raspberry Pi board to the power source via the micro-USB port.

In the following screenshot, you can see the progress of the installation:

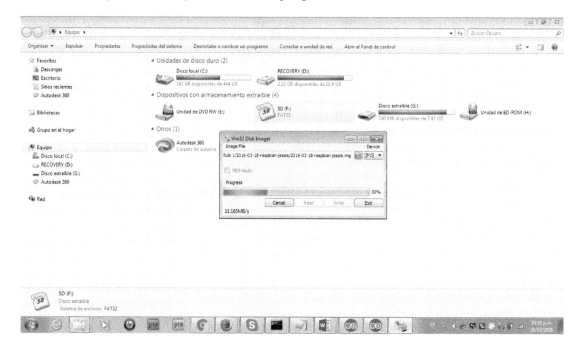

Debugging your Raspberry Pi Zero with a serial console cable

In this section, we will look at how to communicate, the Raspberry Pi Zero from a computer using a TTL serial converter. We can do this debugging with a serial console cable connected to the computer using the USB port. We communicate with the board with a serial cable, because if we want to send commands from our computer to the board, it's necessary to communicate using this cable. You can find the cable at `https://www.adafrui t.com/products/954`:

It's important to consider that the cable uses 3.3 volts, but we don't care because we're using the cable from Adafruit. It is tested to work at this level of voltage.

You need to follow the next steps in order to install and communicate with your Raspberry Pi Zero:

1. It's necessary that you have a free USB port on your computer.
2. We need to install the driver for the serial console cable so that the system can recognize the hardware. We recommend that you download the driver from `https://www.adafruit.com/images/product-files/954/PL2303_Prolific_DriverInstaller_v1_12_0.zip`.
3. We use an interface (console software), called PuTTY, running on a Windows computer; so we can communicate with our board, the Raspberry Pi. This software can be downloaded and installed from `http://www.putty.org/`.
4. For the connections, we need to connect the red cable to **5** volts, the black cable to ground, the white cable to the **TXD** pin, and the green cable to the RXD pin on the Raspberry Pi Zero.
5. The other side of the cable connects the plug to the USB port.

This is an image of the connections; it's for the hardware configuration:

Testing and accessing the serial COM interface

Once the driver is installed, we have here the Port COM, which is already installed:

This configuration is for Windows installation; if you have different operating system, you need to do different steps.

How get the Device Manager screen: On your windows PC, click on the **Start** icon, go to Control Panel, select System, and then click on **Device Manager**.

In the following screenshot, you can see the device manager of the USB serial port:

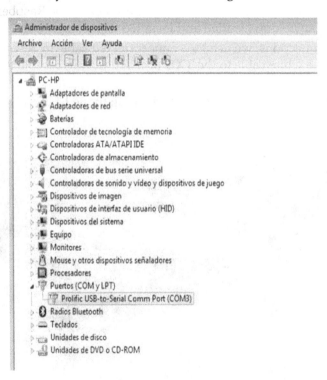

1. Open the terminal in PuTTY, and select Serial Communication as COM3, **Speed** as 115200, **Parity** as **None**, and **Flow Control as None;** click on **Open:**

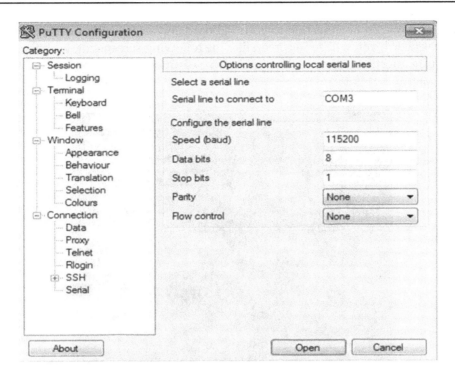

2. When the blank screen appears, press *Enter* on your keyboard:

3. This initiates a connection to your Pi board and asks for your username and password; you will see a screen like the following screenshot, with the authentication login:

4. The default username for the Raspberry Pi Zero is pi, and the password is raspberry:

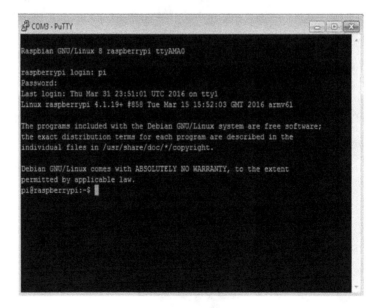

Connecting to the home network and accessing remotely

Our Raspberry Pi will be working in a real network, so it needs to be set up to work with all the devices that will be together. For this reason, we need to configure our home network. We will show you how to use the Ethernet adapter and the Wi-Fi plug that can be used in the Raspberry Pi Zero.

Connecting with an Ethernet adapter

If you want to connect our Raspberry Pi Zero to the local network, you need to use a USB OTG Host Cable – MicroB OTG male to female from Adafruit. You can find it here: `https://www.adafruit.com/products/1099`. The board that we're using doesn't have an Ethernet connector, so it's necessary to use it to communicate with the devices from outside.

In the following image, we can see the Ethernet adapter connected to the Raspberry Pi Zero:

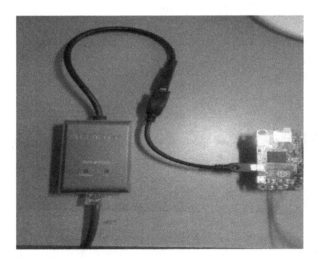

This is the connector that you can use to connect your Ethernet adapter and make a link to the network:

Now we need to follow the next steps to configure the Ethernet connection adapter:

1. Connect your adapter to the converter; I used a **TRENDnet NETAdapter**, but you can use an Ethernet Hub and USB Hub with Micro USB OTG Connector from Adafruit. You can find it here: `https://www.adafruit.com/products/2992m`. This is a hub and can be connected to the Ethernet cable or USB devices.
2. Verify the router configuration, and after both LEDs start blinking, you can see the IP address in your configuration. The DHCP server assigns the IP address to the Raspberry Pi.

This is what you will see as your router configuration on your hostname **raspberrypi**:

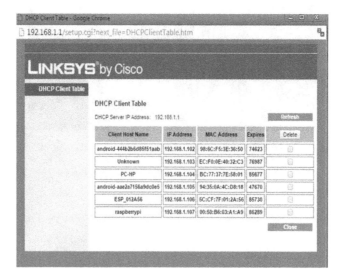

Accessing the Raspberry Pi Zero via SSH

As we know the IP address that our Raspberry Pi has, we will access to it using the PuTTY terminal as we can see in the following screenshot. You need to enter the IP address, and the port is 22 by default; click on the **Open** button:

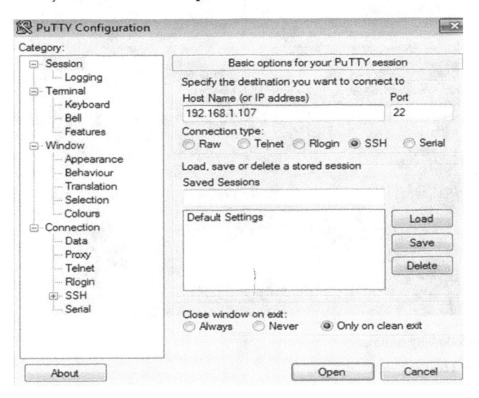

After that, we have the login screen as follows:

Use the following command:

```
sudo ifconfig -a
```

We can now see the information about the configuration of the Ethernet controller adapter. **Eth0** is the Ethernet adapter:

```
pi@raspberrypi ~

Debian GNU/Linux comes with ABSOLUTELY NO WARRANTY, to the extent
permitted by applicable law.
Last login: Fri Mar 18 08:58:23 2016
pi@raspberrypi:~ $ sudo ifconfig -a
eth0      Link encap:Ethernet  HWaddr 00:50:b6:03:a1:a9
          inet addr:192.168.1.107  Bcast:192.168.1.255  Mask:255.255.255.0
          inet6 addr: fe80::12d8:67ba:43b1:e7b2/64 Scope:Link
          UP BROADCAST RUNNING MULTICAST  MTU:1500  Metric:1
          RX packets:161 errors:0 dropped:3 overruns:0 frame:0
          TX packets:155 errors:0 dropped:0 overruns:0 carrier:0
          collisions:0 txqueuelen:1000
          RX bytes:14930 (14.5 KiB)  TX bytes:22275 (21.7 KiB)

lo        Link encap:Local Loopback
          inet addr:127.0.0.1  Mask:255.0.0.0
          inet6 addr: ::1/128 Scope:Host
          UP LOOPBACK RUNNING  MTU:65536  Metric:1
          RX packets:200 errors:0 dropped:0 overruns:0 frame:0
          TX packets:200 errors:0 dropped:0 overruns:0 carrier:0
          collisions:0 txqueuelen:0
          RX bytes:16656 (16.2 KiB)  TX bytes:16656 (16.2 KiB)

pi@raspberrypi:~ $
```

Connecting to the Wi-Fi network

In this section, we will show you how to configure your Wi-Fi network connection so that your Raspberry Pi Zero can interact with your Wi-Fi network. First, we need to connect the Miniature Wi-Fi (802.11b/g/n) Wi-Fi dongle to the Raspberry Pi using the USB OTG Cable:

How to install the wireless tools

Use the following command to configure the wireless network:

```
sudo apt-get install wireless-tools
```

In the following screenshot, we can see the result of the `ifconfig` command:

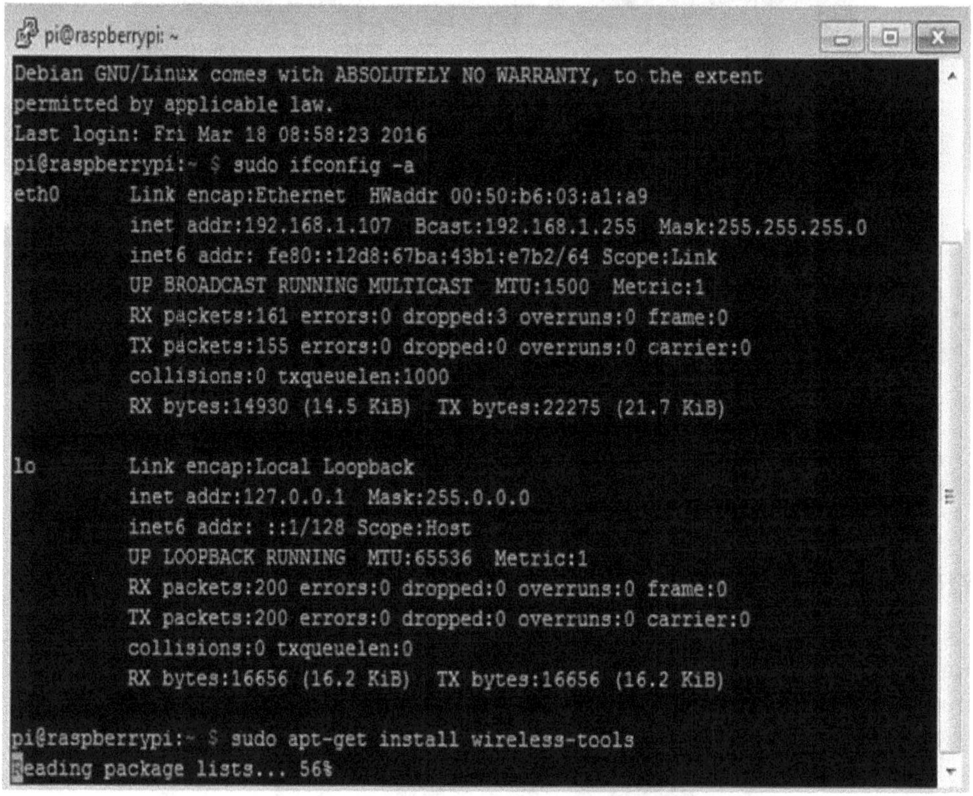

After executing the command, we will see the result of installing `wireless-tools`:

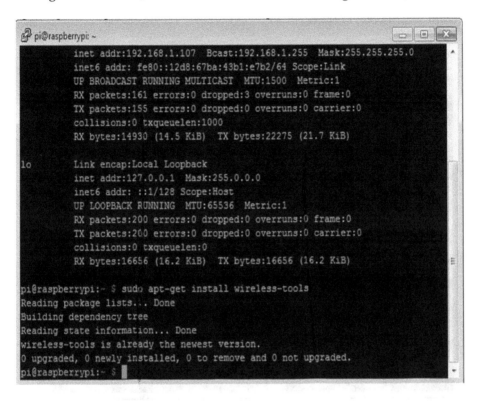

Configuring IP address and wireless network

To have a networking configuration, we need to assign an IP address to our device in order to be involved in the network.

Enter the following command:

```
sudo nano etc/network/interfaces
```

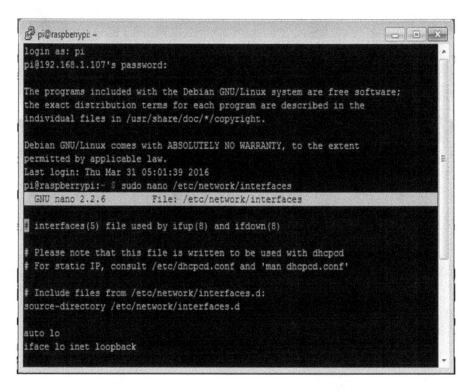

In the following configuration file, called `interface`, we explain what we need to add to the file so that we can connect our Raspberry Pi Zero to the Wi-Fi network for the **Wlan0** connection.

We start the file configuration; it means the beginning of the file:

```
auto lo
```

We configure the Ethernet device `loopback` for the local host and start up the DHCP server:

```
iface lo inet loopback
iface eth0 inet dhcp
```

Allow the configuration of the `wlan0` for Wi-Fi connection:

```
allow-hotplug wlan0
auto wlan0
```

We start up the DHCP server for the Wi-Fi connection and input the name of your `ssid` and the password. We need to type `ssid` and `password` parameters of your Wi-Fi network:

```
iface wlan0 inet dhcp
        wpa-ssid "ssid"
        wpa-psk "password"
```

Testing the communication

We need to test whether the device is responding to the other host. Now, if everything is configured well, we can see the following IP address in the Wi-Fi connection:

```
 pi@raspberrypi: ~

Debian GNU/Linux comes with ABSOLUTELY NO WARRANTY, to the extent
permitted by applicable law.
Last login: Thu Mar 31 05:17:46 2016
pi@raspberrypi:~ $ ifconfig
lo        Link encap:Local Loopback
          inet addr:127.0.0.1  Mask:255.0.0.0
          inet6 addr: ::1/128 Scope:Host
          UP LOOPBACK RUNNING  MTU:65536  Metric:1
          RX packets:72 errors:0 dropped:0 overruns:0 frame:0
          TX packets:72 errors:0 dropped:0 overruns:0 carrier:0
          collisions:0 txqueuelen:0
          RX bytes:6288 (6.1 KiB)  TX bytes:6288 (6.1 KiB)

wlan0     Link encap:Ethernet  HWaddr 40:a5:ef:0c:b2:75
          inet addr:192.168.1.108  Bcast:192.168.1.255  Mask:255.255.255.0
          inet6 addr: fe80::3370:754c:ae3e:d106/64 Scope:Link
          UP BROADCAST RUNNING MULTICAST  MTU:1500  Metric:1
          RX packets:103 errors:0 dropped:15 overruns:0 frame:0
          TX packets:105 errors:0 dropped:1 overruns:0 carrier:0
          collisions:0 txqueuelen:1000
          RX bytes:14942 (14.5 KiB)  TX bytes:19069 (18.6 KiB)

pi@raspberrypi:~ $
```

We can see in the router configuration the current IP address that is assigned to the wireless network:

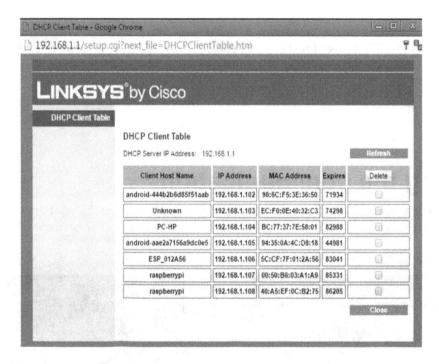

Ping from a computer

Connect the computer to the same network as the Raspberry Pi:

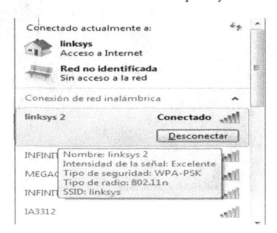

You need to ping the IP address of the Raspberry Pi. After we make the ping to the IP Address of the Raspberry Pi Wireless connection, we see the results:

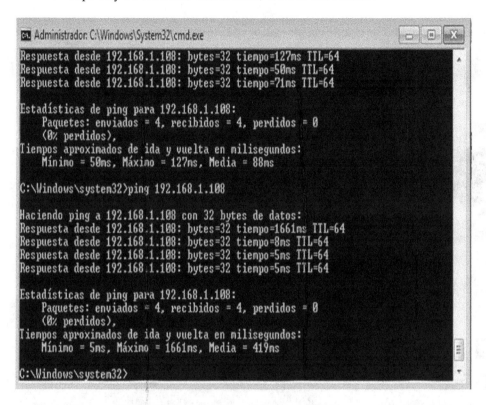

Updating the package repository

This will upgrade your Pi board by downloading all the latest packages from the official Raspberry Pi repository, so it's a great way to make sure that your board is connected to the Internet. Then, from your computer, type the following:

```
sudo apt-get update
```

The following screenshot show the Raspberry Pi collecting the packages data:

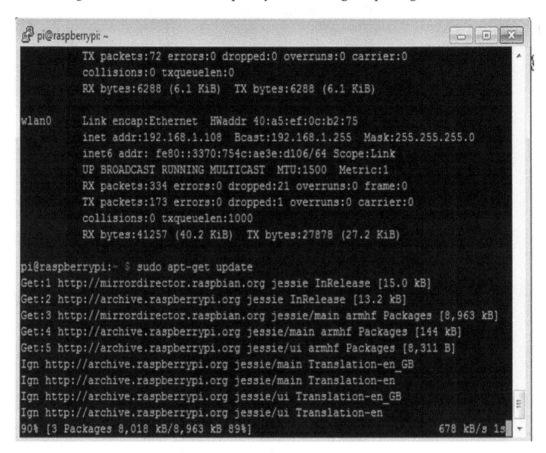

Here we have results after the installation is finished:

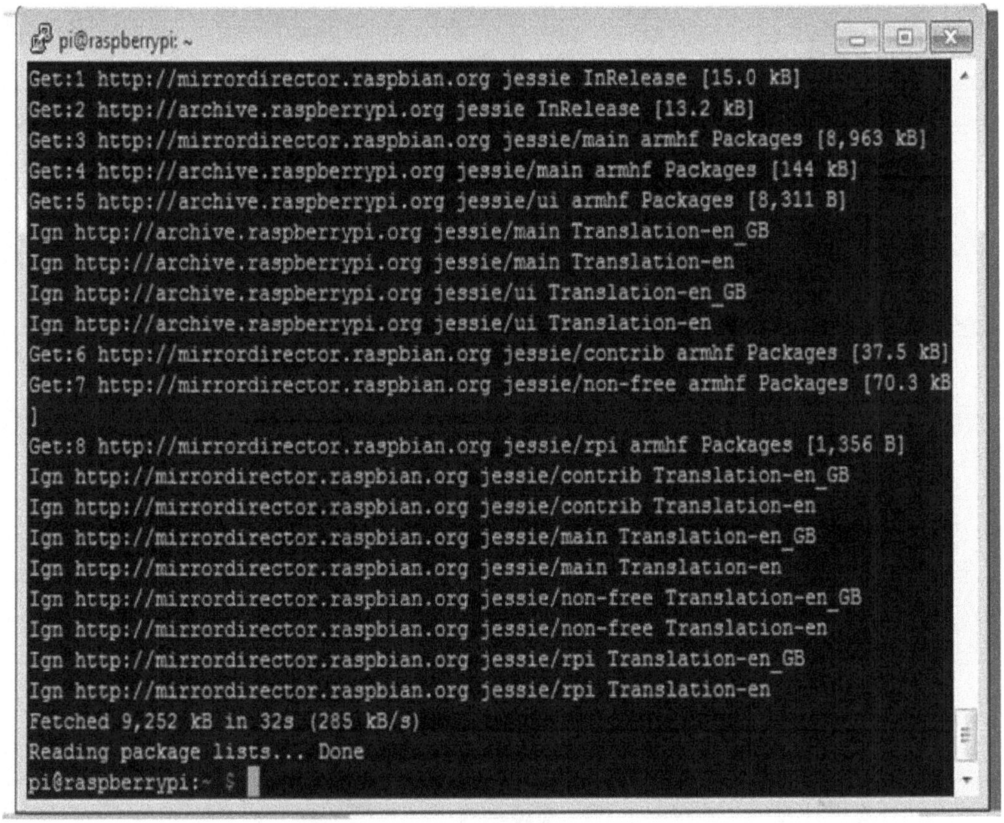

Remote Desktop

In this section, we need the **RDP** package with the Raspbian Operating System. To do that, first we need to execute the following command:

```
sudo apt-get install xrdp
```

This command executes and installs the RDP process and updates the package:

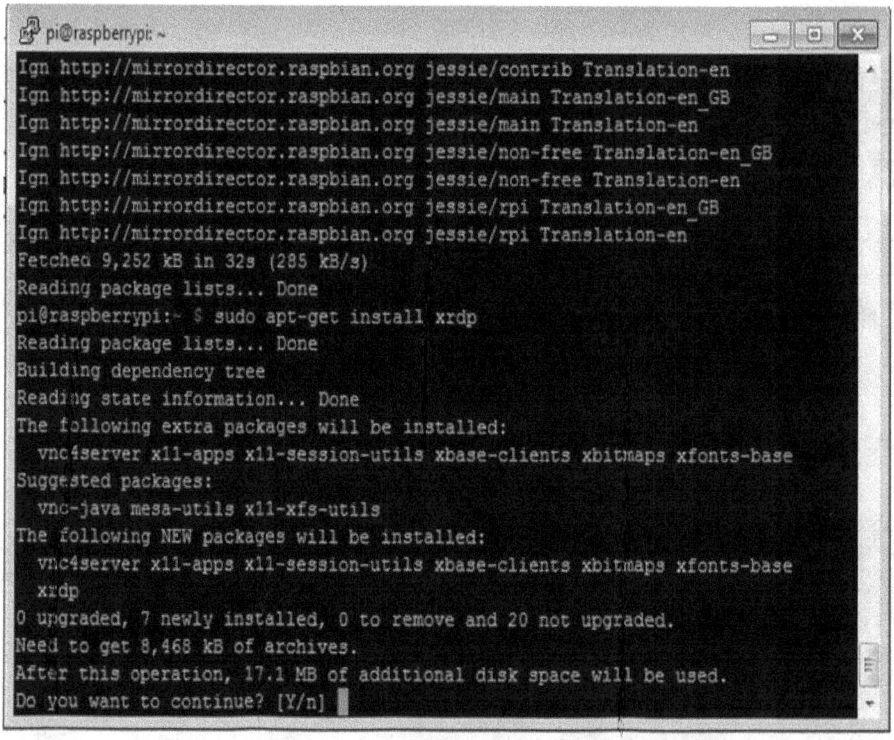

Remote Desktop with Windows

At the end of this chapter, you want to be able to access the board from your own computer using Remote Desktop; you need to type the IP address of your Raspberry Pi and click on the **Connect** button:

After we type the IP address of the Raspberry Pi Zero, we will see the following screen; it's necessary to write your username and password:

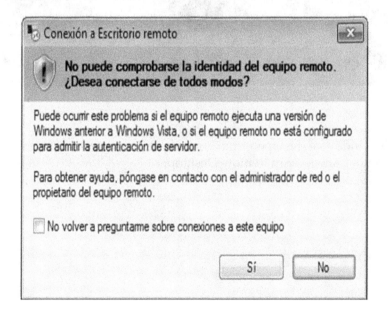

You need the login information of your Raspberry Pi, username, and password:

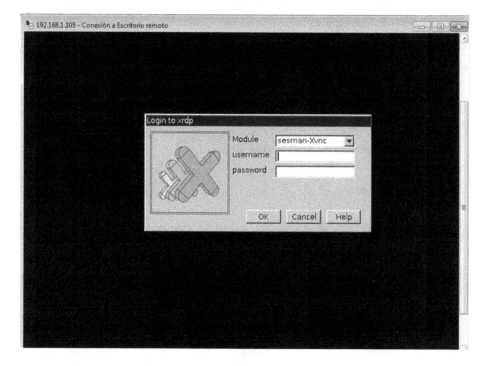

This is the main window of the Operating System; you have correctly accessed your Raspberry Pi Remote Access with Remote Desktop:

Configuring a web server

There are several web servers available that we can install on your Raspberry Pi. We're going to install the lighttpd web server. Also, we need to install PHP support, which will help us run a website into our Raspberry Pi and have dynamic web pages.

To install and configure, log in to the Raspberry Pi via the terminal console of PuTTY:

1. Update the package installer:

   ```
   sudo apt-get update
   ```

2. Install the lighttpd web server:

   ```
   sudo apt-get install lighttpd
   ```

Once installed, it will automatically start up as a background service; it will do so each time the Raspberry Pi starts up:

1. To set up our PHP 5 interface for programming with PHP 5, we need to install the PHP5 module support with the following command; this is necessary to have our server, and it can execute PHP files so that we can make our website:

   ```
   sudo apt-get install php5-cgi
   ```

2. Now we need to enable the PHP FastCGI module on our web server:

   ```
   sudo lighty-enable-mod fastcgi-php
   ```

3. For the last step, we have to restart the server with the following command:

   ```
   sudo /etc/init.d/lighttpd
   ```

In the following screenshot, we show the content of the page that will to appear when we configure the web server and the PHP 5 interface. The web server installs a test placeholder page in the location /var/www. Type the IP address of your Raspberry Pi in the browser, for example, http://192.168.1.105/, and the following screen appears, opening the active page of the configured server:

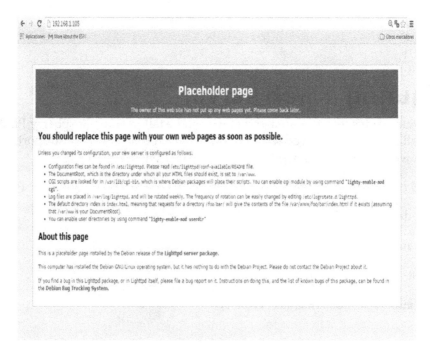

Testing the PHP installation

At this point, we need to test our website with PHP. This can be done by writing a simple PHP script page. If PHP is installed correctly, it will return information about its environment and configuration.

1. Go to the next folder, where it's the root document:

   cd /var/www/html

2. Create a file called phpinfo.php.

   We use the word nano so that we can get into the file of the system with the privileges and execute the following command:

   sudo nano phpinfo.php

3. After creating the file, as given in the following screenshot, press *CTRL-X*, and then save the file:

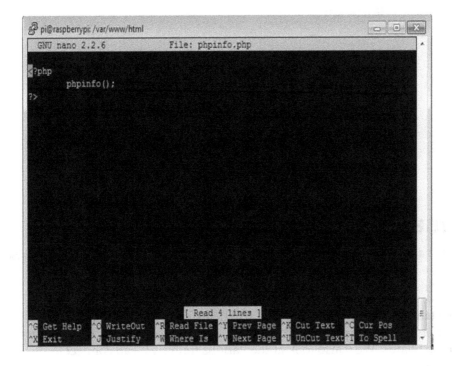

4. In your browser, enter the IP address of your Raspberry Pi, for example, `http://192.168.1.105/phpinfo.php`, and you should see the following screen:

Summary

In the first chapter of this book, we looked at how to configure our Raspberry Pi Zero board so we can use it in later chapters. We looked at what components were needed for the Pi, and how to install Raspbian so we can run the software on our board.

We also installed a web server, which we will be using in some projects of the book. In the following chapter, we are going to dive into how to connect devices to your Raspberry Pi and Arduino boards. We'll also look at the various things we can connect to the Raspberry Pi using GPIO.

2
Connecting Things to the Raspberry Pi Zero

You need to learn how to connect things to your Raspberry Pi Zero, and also looked at the architecture and differentiate between the pins we can use for the purpose we defined. This is the reason we have this section–to help you with the sensors we can connect and give the basics of how to connect other things to your device. In this section, we will explain how to configure the Raspberry Pi; now you cannot avoid learning how to connect to your Raspberry Pi sensors to read analog inputs connected to it.

We will cover the following topics to make our hardware communicate with the board:

- Connecting digital inputs: Sensor DS18B20
- Connecting analog inputs using an MCP3008 ADC converter
- Connecting a real–time clock (RTC)

Connectting digital input – sensor DS18B20

The Raspberry Pi has digital pins, so in this section, we will look at how to connect a digital sensor to the board. We will use the digital sensor DS18B20, which has a digital output and can be perfectly connected to a digital input in our Raspberry Pi sensor. The main idea is to take temperature readings from the sensor and display them on the screen.

Hardware requirements

We will require the following hardware to take the temperature reading:

- Temperature sensor DS18B20 (waterproof)
- One resistor of 4.7 kilo-ohms
- Some jumper wires
- A breadboard

We will use a waterproof sensor DS18B20 and a 4.7 kilo-ohm resistor:

This is the waterproof sensor that we are using in this project.

Hardware connections

The following diagram shows the circuit on the breadboard, with the sensor and the resistor:

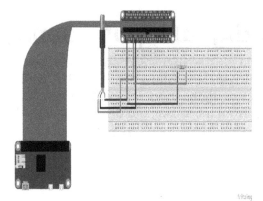

In the following image, we can see the circuit with the sensor:

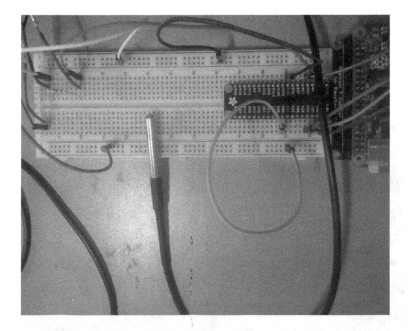

Configuring the one-wire protocol

Open a terminal in the Raspberry Pi, and type the following:

```
sudo nano /boot/config.txt
```

You should type the following line at the bottom of the page to configure the protocol and define the pin where the one-wire protocol will communicate:

```
dtoverlay=w1-gpio
```

The next step is to reboot the Raspberry Pi. After a few minutes, open the terminal and type the following lines:

```
sudo modprobew1-gpio
sudo modprobe w1-therm
```

Enter the folder and select the device that will be configured:

```
cd /sys/bus/w1/devices
ls
```

Select the device that will be set up. Change xxxx to the serial number of the device that will set up in the protocol:

```
cd 28-xxxx
cat w1_slave
```

You will see the following:

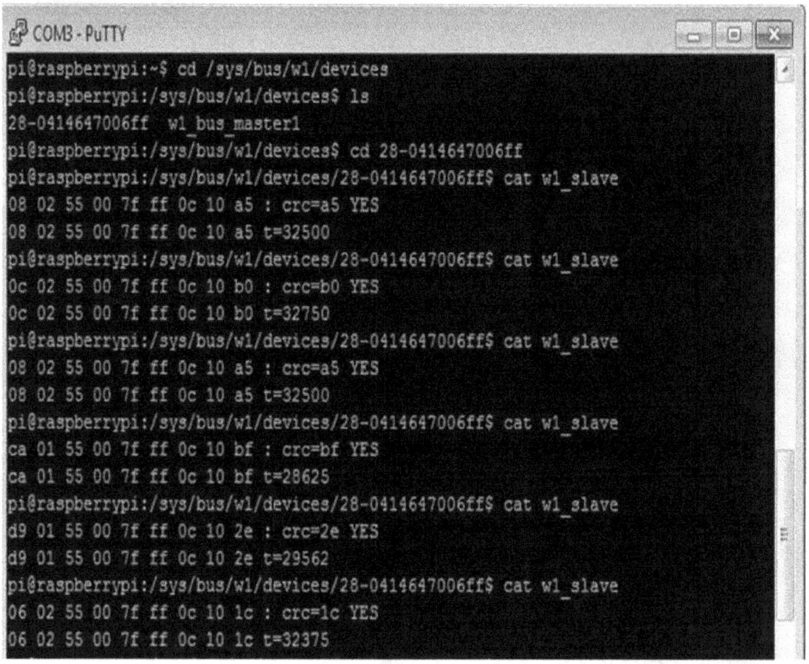

After that, you will see one line which says *Yes if it appears that the temperature reading is done like this: t=29.562.*

Software configuration

Let's now look at the code to display the temperature in degrees Celsius and Fahrenheit every second on the screen.

Here we import the libraries used in the program:

```
import os1
import glob1
import time1
```

Here we define the devices configured in the protocol:

```
os1.system('modprobew1-gpio')
os1.system('modprobew1-therm1')
```

Here we define the folders where the devices are configured:

```
directory = '/sys/bus/w1/devices/'
device_folder1 = glob1.glob(directory + '28*')[0]
device_file1 = device_folder1 + '/w1_slave'
```

Then we define the functions to read `temperature` and configure the sensor:

```
defread_temp():
f = open(device_file1, 'r')
readings = f.readlines()
f.close()
return readings
```

Read the temperature with the function:

```
defread_temp():
readings = read_temp()
```

In this function, we compare when it received the message `YES` and get the `t=` character. We also get the value of the temperature:

```
while readings[0].strip()[-3:] != 'YES':
time1.sleep(0.2)
readings = read_temp()
equals = lines[1].find('t=')
```

Then we calculate the temperature, `temp` in `C` and `F`, and return the values:

```
if equals != -1:
temp = readings[1][equals pos+2:]
tempc = float(temp) / 1000.0
tempf = temp * 9.0 / 5.0 + 32.0
returntempc, tempf
```

It repeats the cycle every second:

```
while True:
print(temp())
time1.sleep(1)
```

Displaying the readings on the screen

Now we need to execute `thermometer.py`. To show the results of the scripts made in Python, open your PuTTY terminal, and type the following command:

```
sudo python thermometer.py
```

The command means that, when we run the thermometer file, if everything is running perfectly, we will see the following results:

Connecting analog inputs using an MCP3008 ADC Converter

If we want to connect analog sensors to the Raspberry Pi, we need to use an **Analog-to-Digital Converter** (**ADC**). The board doesn't have analog inputs; we use the **MCP3008** to connect analog sensors. This is a 10-bit ADC and has eight channels. This means that you can connect up to eight sensors that can be read from the Raspberry Pi Zero. We don't need special components to connect them. They can be connected with SPI to the Raspberry Pi's GPIOs.

The first step is to enable SPI communication:

1. Access the Raspberry Pi terminal and type the following command:

    ```
    sudo raspi-config
    ```

2. Select **Advanced Options,** as shown in the following screenshot:

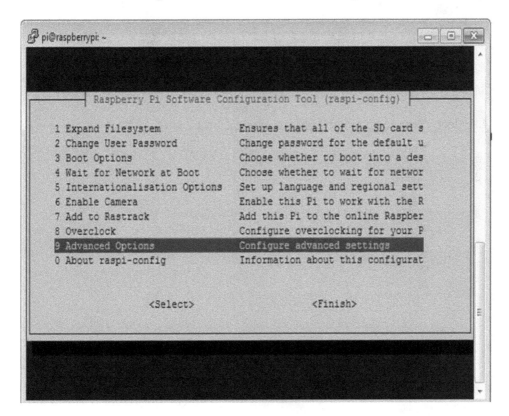

3. Enable **SPI** communication by selecting the **SPI** option:

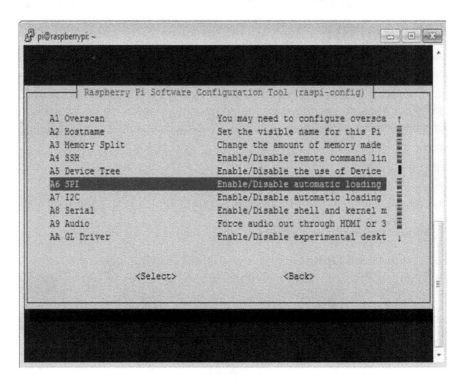

4. Select **<Yes>** to enable the SPI interface:

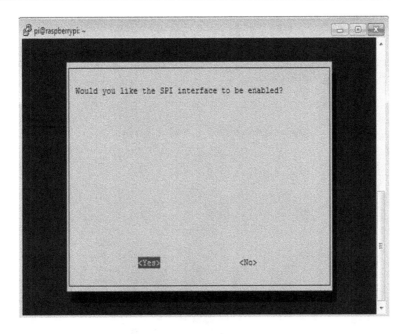

5. The final screen looks like the following screenshot when we enable the SPI interface. Select **<Ok>**:

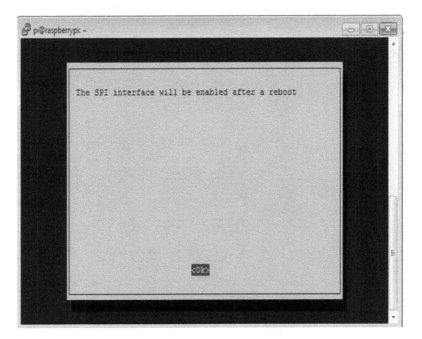

Raspberry Pi GPIO header

The following screenshot is a chart of the GPIO pins of the Raspberry Pi Zero. In this case, we will use the SPI configuration interface (SPI_MOSI, SPI_MISO, SPI_CLK, SPI_CE0_N):

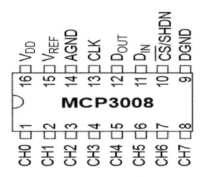

The following diagram shows the name of the pins of the MCP3008 chip that you connect to the Raspberry Pi:

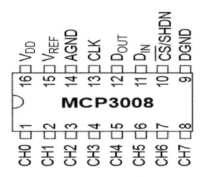

The following image shows the temperature sensor:

You need to connect the following pins according to the next description:

- **VDD** to 3.3 volts
- **VREF** to **3.3** volts from the Raspberry Pi Zero
- Pin **AGND** to **GND**
- Pin **CLK** (clock) to **GPIO11** of the Raspberry Pi
- **DOUT** to **GPIO9**
- Pin **DIN** to **GPIO10**
- Pin **CS** to **GPIO8** and the pin
- Pin the MCP3008D **GND** to Ground

This connection is represented in the following figure:

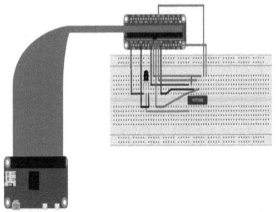

The following image shows the connections of the sensor to the ADC MCP3008 and the Raspberry Pi:

Reading the data with a Python script

In the next section, you will create the MCP3008.py file; you need to follow the next steps:

1. Open the terminal on your Raspberry Pi Zero.
2. Enter the interface in your Pi terminal.
3. It's important to use nano before.
4. Type sudo nano MCP3008.py.

It will appear on the screen and we will describe the following lines:

1. Import libraries:

    ```
    import spidev1
    import os1
    ```

2. Open the SPI bus:

    ```
    spi1 = spidev1.SpiDev1()
    spi1.open(0,0)
    ```

3. Define the channels from the ADC MCP2008:

```
def ReadChannel1(channel1):
   adc1 = spi1.xfer2([1,(8+channel1)<<4,0])
   data1 = ((adc1[1]&3) << 8) + adc1[2]
   return data1
```

4. The function to convert volts is as follows:

```
def volts(data1,places1):
   volts1 = (data1 * 3.3) / float(1023)
   volts1 = round(volts1,places1)
   return volts1
```

5. The function to convert temperature is as follows:

```
def Temp(data1,places1):
   temp1 = (data1 * 0.0032)*100
   temp1 = round(temp1,places1)
   return temp1
```

6. Define channels from the ADC:

```
channels = 0
```

7. Define the reading time:

```
delay = 10
```

8. The function to read the temperature is as follows:

```
while True:

   temp  = Channels(temp)
   volts = Volts(temp1,2)
   temp  = Temp(temp1,2)
```

9. Print the results:

```
print"************************************************"
print("Temp : {} ({}V) {} degC".format(temp1,volts,temp))
```

10. Wait every 5 seconds:

```
Time1.sleep(delay)
```

11. Run the Python file using the following command:

```
sudo python MCP3008.py
```

12. On the following screen, we can see the temperature, the ADC measurements, and the volts according to the temperature:

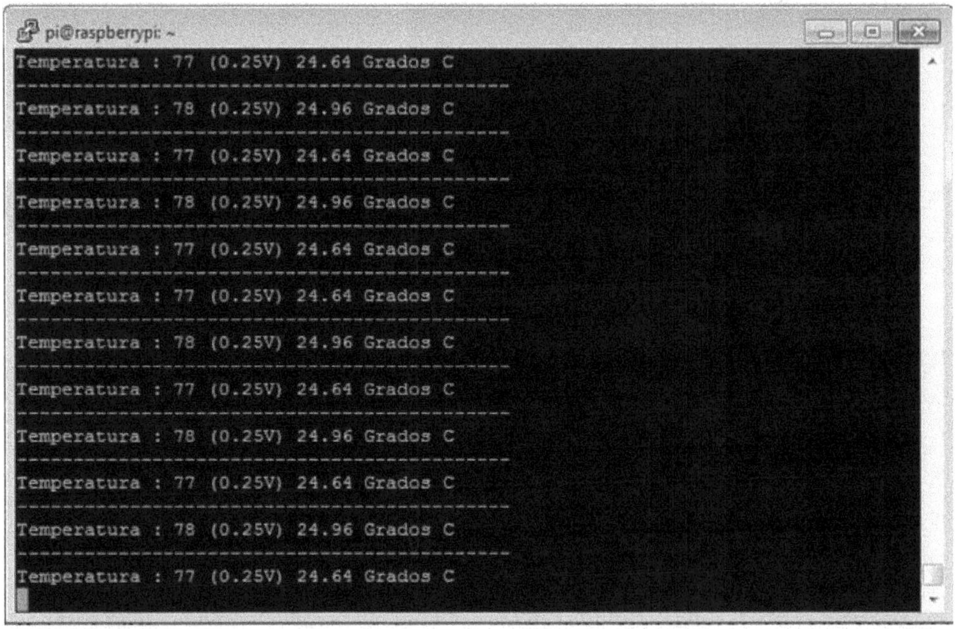

Connecting an RTC

To control a system, it is very important to have a circuit that can read the time; it can help control the outputs from the Raspberry Pi or detect an action at a specific time. We will interface an **RTC** module *DS3231* with the Raspberry Pi.

I2C setup

The first step is to enable the **I2C** interface by performing the following steps:

1. Select **Advanced Options**:

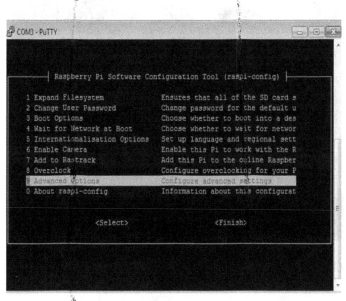

2. Enable the **I2C** option, as shown in the following screenshot:

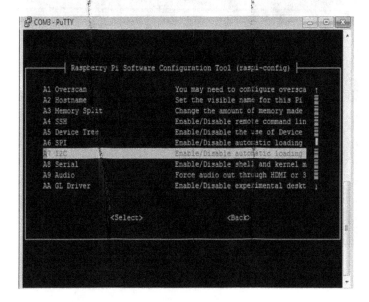

3. Select **<Yes>** on the next screen:

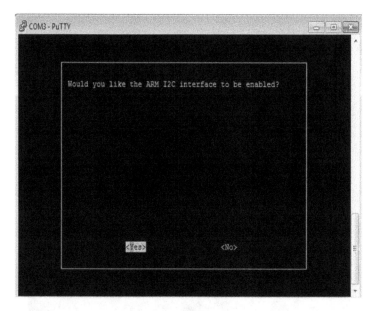

4. Select **<Ok>**:

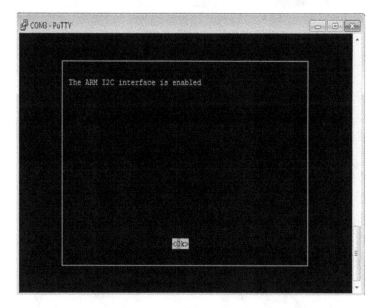

5. Then select **<Yes>**:

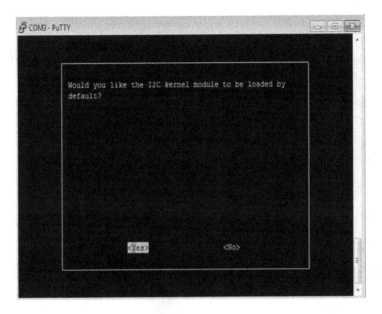

6. Next, select **<OK>**:

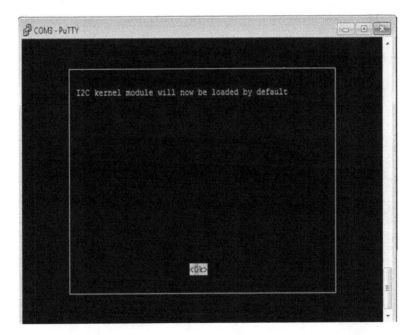

DS3231 module setup

The module DS3231 is a real-time clock. It can be used to get the time and date from an integrated circuit, so it can work with your system to control specific events that you want to program from an embedded chip. It can work perfectly with the Raspberry Pi Zero in order to get the time and date in real time.

You need to be sure that you have the latest updates. To do that, type the following commands in your terminal:

```
sudo apt-get update
sudo apt-get -y upgrade
```

Modify the system file with the following command:

```
sudo nano /etc/modules
```

Add the following lines to the modules.txt file:

```
snd-bcm2835
i2c-bcm2835
i2c-dev
rtc-ds1307
```

Hardware setup

In this section, we will look at the pins of the RTC module:

```
DS3231    Pi GPIO
GNDP      1-06
VCC       (3.3V)
SDA       (I2CSDA)
SCL       (I2CSCL)
```

This is the RTC module, and we can see the pins of the chip:

The following diagram shows, the circuit connection:

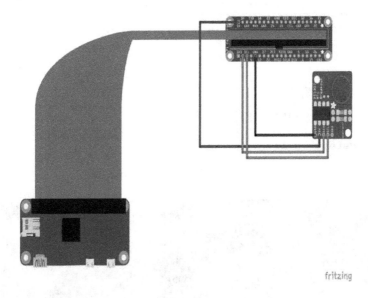

The following image shows the final connection:

Testing the RTC

Open the terminal, and type this:

```
sudo i2cdetect -y 1
```

You should see something similar to the following screenshot:

```
pi@raspberrypi:~$ sudo i2cdetect -y 1
     0  1  2  3  4  5  6  7  8  9  a  b  c  d  e  f
00:          -- -- -- -- -- -- -- -- -- -- -- --
10: -- -- -- -- -- -- -- -- -- -- -- -- -- -- -- --
20: -- -- -- -- -- -- -- -- -- -- -- -- -- -- -- --
30: -- -- -- -- -- -- -- -- -- -- -- -- -- -- -- --
40: -- -- -- -- -- -- -- -- -- -- -- -- -- -- -- --
50: -- -- -- -- -- -- -- 57 -- -- -- -- -- -- -- --
60: -- -- -- -- -- -- -- -- 68 -- -- -- -- -- -- --
70: -- -- -- -- -- -- -- --
pi@raspberrypi:~$
```

I2C device setup

The next step is to check whether the time clock is synchronized with RTC time. Here we define the RTC local:

```
sudo nano /etc/rc.local
```

Add the following lines to the file as we declare the new device and the path we configure:

```
echo ds1307 0x68 > /sys/class/i2c-adapter/i2c-1/new_device
```

The following command will start up the RTC:

```
hwclock -s
```

After this command, reboot the Pi. You will see the following screen, which means that the RTC is configured and ready to work:

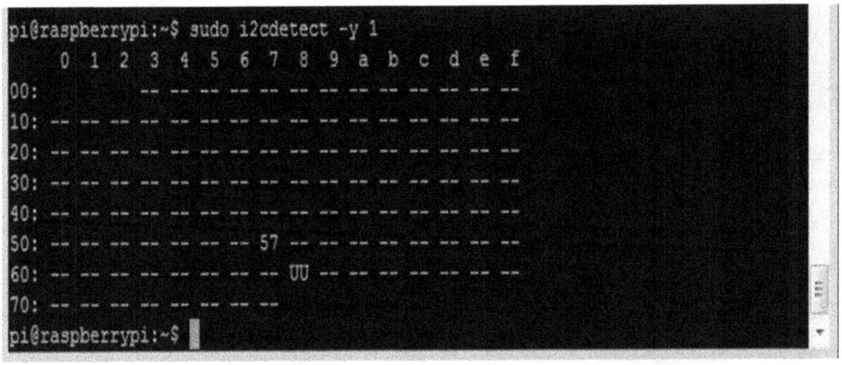

Putting the real-time clock to final test

You can read the Pi time system with the following command:

```
date
```

Once the RTC is ready, you can test it with the following command; write the time to the RTC:

```
sudo hwclock -w
```

You can read the time from the RTC with the command given here:

```
sudo hwclock -r
```

Now for the final command. With this command, we can see both the time values, as shown in the following screenshot:

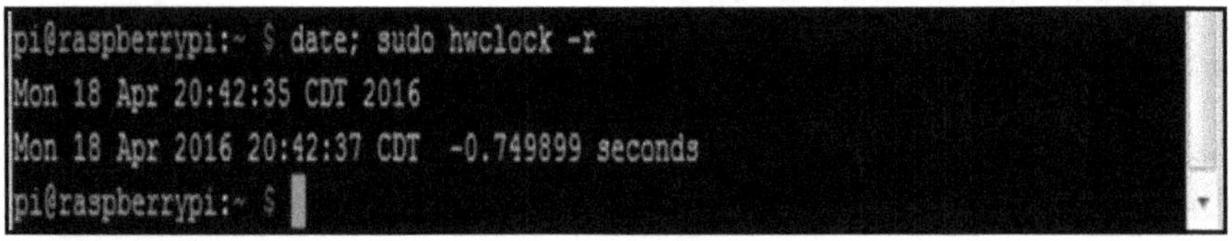

```
pi@raspberrypi:~ $ date; sudo hwclock -r
Mon 18 Apr 20:42:35 CDT 2016
Mon 18 Apr 2016 20:42:37 CDT  -0.749899 seconds
pi@raspberrypi:~ $
```

Summary

In this chapter, you learned how to use the MCP3008 ADC converter and also how to use a temperature sensor using Raspberry Pi Zero. We explored the GPIO port and the various interfaces it features. We looked at the various things we can connect to the Raspberry Pi using GPIO.

In the next chapter, we will dive into more hardware acquisition, connecting different kinds of sensors to our Raspberry Pi Zero and Arduino boards. This will help you make real measurements in your projects. That's very interesting–keep at it!

3
Connecting Sensors - Measure the Real Things

The objectives of this book are to build a Home Security System, control domestic appliances by electronically controlled systems with sensors, and monitor them from a dashboard. First, we need to consider that our sensors are connected to an end device that can read the signals and transmit them to the network.

For the end devices, we will use Arduino boards to acquire the readings from the sensors. We can see that the Raspberry Pi doesn't have analog inputs. For this reason, we use an Arduino board to read that signals.

In the previous chapter, we talked about how to connect devices to the Raspberry Pi; in this section, we will see how to interface sensors with Arduino boards to see how to read real signals from different applications for real measurements. We will cover the following topics in this chapter:

- Using a flow sensor to calculate the volume of water
- Measuring the concentration of gas with a sensor
- Measuring the level of alcohol with a sensor
- Detecting fire with a sensor
- Measuring the humidity for plants
- Measuring the level of water in a recipient
- Measuring temperature, humidity and light and display data in an LCD
- Detecting motion with a PIR sensor
- Detecting if the door is open with a reed switch
- Detecting who can get in the house with a fingerprint sensor

It's important to consider the fact that we need to communicate our system to the real world. Since we are working on building a home security system, we need to learn how to connect and interact with some necessary sensors to use them in our system.

In the next section, we will cover the sensors that you will need to read the data you use in the domotics and security system.

Measuring flow sensor to calculate the volume of water

We need to take automatic measurements from the water that we're using in the home. For this project, we will use a sensor to perform this reading and make the reading of measurement automatic.

To make this project, we need the following materials:

Flow Water Sensor and Arduino UNO board:

Hardware connections

Now we have the connections for out flow sensor. We can see that it has three pins — the red pin is connected to **+VCC 5** volts, the black one is connected to **GND,** and the yellow pin is connected to pin number **2** of the Arduino board as seen in the following image:

Reading the sensor signal

An interrupt is used for the pulses generated by the passage of water to be accounted as follows:

```
attachInterrupt(0, count_pulse, RISING);
```

The interruption is of type RISING counts the pulses that pass from a low state to a high:

Function for counting pulses:

```
voidcount_pulse()
{
pulse++;
}
```

Reading and counting pulses with Arduino

In this part of the code, we explain that it counts the signals from the sensor using an interrupt, executes, and we have configured it as RISING, so it counts the pulses from digital signal zero to digital signal one:

```
int pin = 2;
volatile unsigned int pulse;
constintpulses_per_litre = 450;

void setup()
{
Serial.begin(9600);

pinMode(pin, INPUT);
attachInterrupt(0, count_pulse, RISING);
```

```
}

void loop()
{
pulse=0;
interrupts();
delay(1000);
noInterrupts();

Serial.print("Pulses per second: ");
Serial.println(pulse);
}

voidcount_pulse()
{
pulse++;
}
```

Open the Arduino Serial Monitor, and blow air through the water flow sensor using your mouth. The number of pulses per second will be printed on the Arduino Serial Monitor for each loop, as shown in the following screenshot:

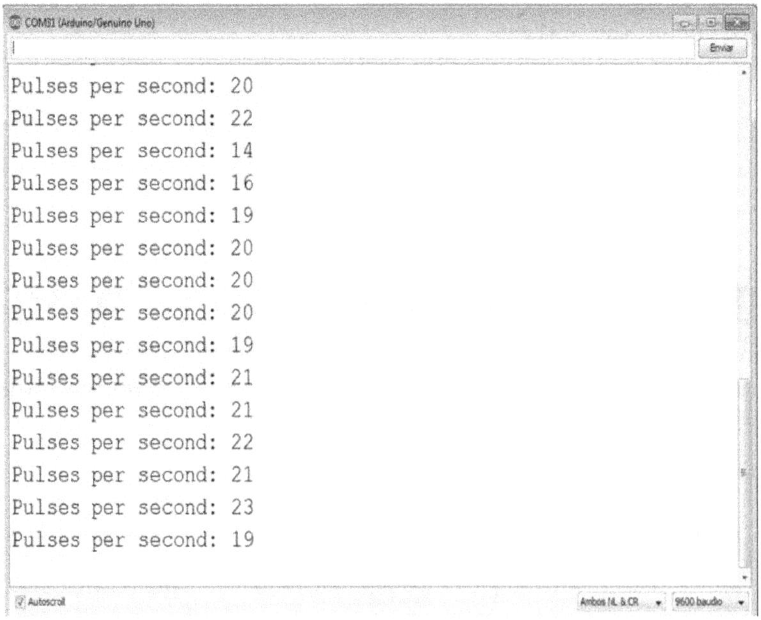

Calculating water flow rate based on the pulses counted

In this part, we measure the pulses and convert them to the flow of water using the following steps:

1. Open a new Arduino IDE, and copy the following sketch.
2. Verify and upload the sketch on the Arduino board.

```
int pin = 2;
volatile unsigned int pulse;
constintpulses_per_litre = 450;

void setup()
{
   Serial.begin(9600);

   pinMode(pin, INPUT);
   attachInterrupt(0, count_pulse, RISING);
}
```

3. The following code will calculate the pulses that are reading from the sensor; we divide the number of pulses counted in one second, and we have pulses per liter:

```
void loop()
{
  pulse = 0;
  interrupts();
  delay(1000);
  noInterrupts();

  Serial.print("Pulses per second: ");
  Serial.println(pulse);

  Serial.print("Water flow rate: ");
  Serial.print(pulse * 1000/pulses_per_litre);
  Serial.println(" milliliters per second");
  delay(1000);
}
void count_pulse()
{
  pulse++;
}
```

4. Open the Arduino Serial Monitor, and blow air through the water flow sensor using your mouth. The number of pulses per second and the water flow rate in milliliters per second will be printed on the Arduino Serial Monitor for each loop, as shown in the following screenshot:

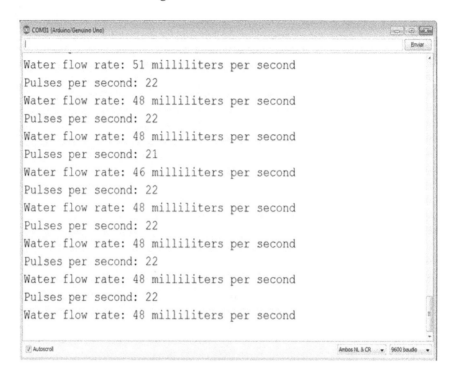

Calculating flow and volume of water:

You can now either copy the code inside a file called Flow_sensor_measure_volume.ino, or just get the complete code from the folder for this project.

In this part, we calculate the flow and volume from the sensor:

```
int pin = 2;
volatile unsigned int pulse;
float volume = 0;
floatflow_rate =0;
constintpulses_per_litre = 450;
```

We set up the interrupt:

```
void setup()
{
Serial.begin(9600);
pinMode(pin, INPUT);
attachInterrupt(0, count_pulse, RISING);
}
```

Start the interrupt:

```
void loop()
{
pulse=0;
interrupts();
delay(1000);
noInterrupts();
```

Then we display the flow rate of the sensor:

```
Serial.print("Pulses per second: ");
Serial.println(pulse);

flow_rate = pulse * 1000/pulses_per_litre;
```

We calculate the volume of the sensor:

```
Serial.print("Water flow rate: ");
Serial.print(flow_rate);
Serial.println(" milliliters per second");

volume = volume + flow_rate * 0.1;
```

We display the volume in milliliters:

```
Serial.print("Volume: ");
Serial.print(volume);
Serial.println(" milliliters");
}
```

The function to count the pulses is as follows:

```
Void count_pulse()
{
  pulse++;
}
```

The result can be seen in the following screenshot:

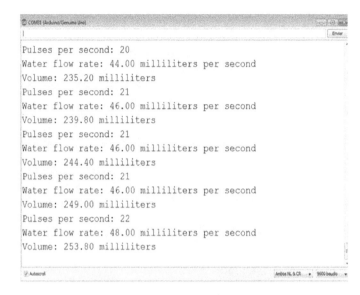

Displaying the parameters measured on an LCD

You can add an LCD screen to your newly built water meter to display readings rather than displaying them on the Arduino serial monitor. You can then disconnect your water meter from the computer after uploading the sketch onto your Arduino.

First, we define the LCD library:

```
#include <LiquidCrystal.h>
```

Then we define the variables that we will use in the program:

```
int pin = 2;
volatile unsigned int pulse;
float volume = 0;
floatflow_rate = 0;
constintpulses_per_litre = 450;
```

We define the LCD pins:

```
// initialize the library with the numbers of the interface pins
LiquidCrystallcd(12, 11, 6, 5, 4, 3);
```

We define the interrupt for sensing:

```
void setup()
{
   Serial.begin(9600);
   pinMode(pin, INPUT);
   attachInterrupt(0, count_pulse, RISING);
```

Now we display the message on LCD:

```
   // set up the LCD's number of columns and rows:
   lcd.begin(16, 2);
   // Print a message to the LCD.
   lcd.print("Welcome...");
   delay(1000);
}
```

We now define the interrupt in the main loop:

```
void loop()
{
   pulse = 0;

   interrupts();
   delay(1000);
   noInterrupts();
```

We display the value on the LCD:

```
   lcd.setCursor(0, 0);
   lcd.print("Pulses/s: ");
   lcd.print(pulse);

   flow_rate = pulse*1000/pulses_per_litre;
```

Then we display the value of the flow rate:

```
   lcd.setCursor(0, 1);
   lcd.print(flow_rate,2);//display only 2 decimal places
   lcd.print(" ml");
```

We now display the value of the volume:

```
   volume = volume + flow_rate * 0.1;
   lcd.setCursor(8, 1);
   lcd.print(volume, 2);//display only 2 decimal places
   lcd.println(" ml ");
}
```

Then we define the function for counting the pulses:

```
void count_pulse()
{
 pulse++;
}
```

Connections with the water flow are shown in the following image:

The following picture shows the measurements on an LCD:

You can see some information on the LCD screen, such as pulses per second, water flow rate, and the total volume of water from the beginning of the time.

Measuring the concentration of gas

It's important to have in our system a sensor that detects gas so we can apply it in our home in order to detect a gas leak. Now we're going to describe how to connect to an Arduino board and read the concentration of gas.

In this section, we will use a gas sensor and Methane CH4. In this case, we will use an MQ-4 sensor that can detect concentrations from 200 to 10000 ppm.

This sensor has an analog resistance in its output and can connect to an ADC; it needs a coil energize of 5 volts. The image for the sensor can be seen as follows:

We can find information for the MQ-4 sensor at https://www.sparkfun.com/products/9404.

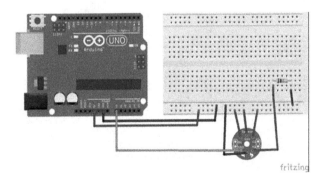

Connections with the sensor and Arduino board

According to the preceding diagram, we will now see the connections made in the following image:

Open the Arduino IDE, and copy the following sketch:

```
void setup(){
  Serial.begin(9600);
}

void loop()
{
  float vol;
  int sensorValue = analogRead(A0);
  vol=(float)sensorValue/1024*5.0;
  Serial.println(vol,1);
  Serial.print("Concentration of gas= ");
  Serial.println(sensorValue);
  delay(2000);
}
```

We see the following results on the screen:

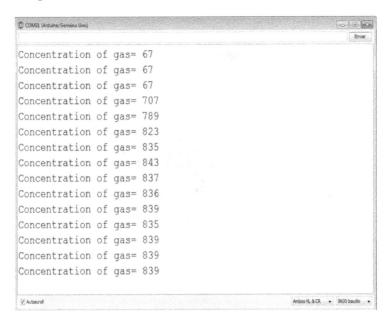

Measuring the level of alcohol with a sensor

In this section, we will build a very cool project: Your very own **Alcohol Breath Analyser**. To do that, we are going to use a simple Arduino Uno board along with an ethanol gas sensor:

The following diagram shows the connection of the sensor with the Arduino:

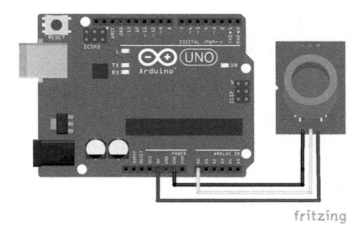

We are now going to write the code for the project. Here, we are simply going to go over the most important parts of the code.

You can now either copy the code inside a file called `Sensor_alcohol.ino`, or just get the complete code from the folder for this project:

```
int readings=0;
void setup(){
Serial.begin(9600);
}

void loop(){
lectura=analogRead(A1);
Serial.print("Level of alcohol= ");
Serial.println(readings);
delay(1000);
}
```

When it doesn't detect alcohol, we can see the number of values that the Arduino reads:

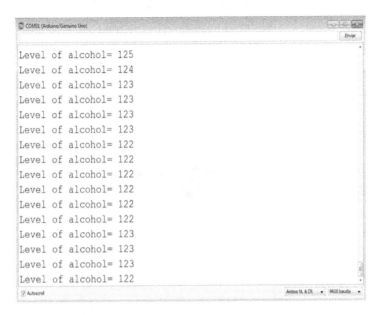

If it detects alcohol, we see values from the analog read from Arduino as shown in the following screenshot:

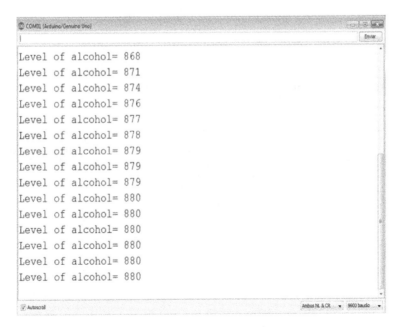

Detecting fire with a sensor

If there's a fire in our home, it's vital to detect it; so in the next section, we will create a project that detects fire with a sensor.

In the following image, we see of the fire sensor module:

You can now either copy the code inside a file called `Sensor_fire.ino`, or just get the complete code from the folder for this project.

We define the variables for our program at the beginning:

```
int ledPin = 13;
int inputPin= 2;
int val = 0;
```

We define the output signals and the serial communication:

```
void setup() {
pinMode(ledPin, OUTPUT);
pinMode(inputPin, INPUT);
Serial.begin(9600);
}
```

Now we display the value of the digital signal:

```
void loop(){
val = digitalRead(inputPin);
Serial.print("val : ");
Serial.println(val);
digitalWrite(ledPin, HIGH);  // turn LED ON
```

Then we compare: If the value detects a high logic state, it turns off the output; if it reads the opposite, it turns on the digital signal; this means that it has detected fire:

```
if (val == HIGH) {
  Serial.print("NO Fire detected ");
  digitalWrite(ledPin, LOW); // turn LED OFF
}
else{
  Serial.print("Fire DETECTED ");
  digitalWrite(ledPin, HIGH);
  }
}
```

When the Arduino board detects fire, it will read *1* in the digital input, which means no fire detection:

If it detects fire, the digital input reads *0* logic from the digital input:

Measuring the humidity for plants

In this section, we will see the testing of humidity inside a plant and the soil using a sensor:

I will now go through the main parts of this first piece of code. Then we set up the serial communication:

```
int value;

void setup() {
Serial.begin(9600);
}
```

In the main loop, we will read the analog signal from the sensor:

```
void loop(){
Serial.print("Humidity sensor value:");
Value = analogRead(0);
Serial.print(value);
```

We compare the value of the sensor and display the result on the serial interface:

```
if (Value<= 300)
Serial.println(" Very wet");
if ((Value > 300) and (Value<= 700))
Serial.println(" Wet, do not water");
if (Value> 700)
Serial.println(" Dry, you need to water");
delay(1000);
}
```

Here, the screenshot shows the results of the readings:

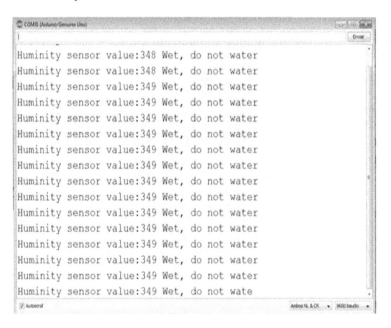

The following screenshot shows that the plant doesn't require water; because it has enough moisture in the soil already:

Measuring the level of water in a recipient

Somtimes, we need to measure the level of water in a recipient, or if you want to see the level of water in a tank, it is a requirement to measure the levels of water that it has; so in this section, we will explain how to do this.

The sensor is Normally Open. When the water is over the limit, the contact opens, and it sends a signal to the Arduino board. We use pin number 2, which is a digital input:

We declare the variables and const in the program:

```
const int buttonPin = 2;      // the number of the input sensor pin
const int ledPin =  13;       // the number of the LED pin
```

We also define the states of the digital signals:

```
// variables will change:
intbuttonState = 0;           // variable for reading the pushbutton status
```

We configure the signals of the program, inputs, and outputs:

```
void setup() {
  // initialize the LED pin as an output:
pinMode(ledPin, OUTPUT);
  // initialize the pushbutton pin as an input:
pinMode(buttonPin, INPUT);
Serial.begin(9600);
}
```

We read the state of the digital input:

```
void loop() {
   // read the state of the pushbutton value:
buttonState = digitalRead(buttonPin);
```

We make the comparisons for the sensor:

```
if (buttonState == HIGH) {
Serial.println(buttonState);
Serial.println("The recipient is fulled");
digitalWrite(ledPin, HIGH);
delay(1000);
   }
```

If the sensor detects a **LOW** level, the recipient is empty:

```
else {
digitalWrite(ledPin, LOW);
Serial.println(buttonState);
Serial.println("The recipient is empty");
delay(1000);
   }
}
```

The following screenshot shows the result when the recipient is empty:

The water is over the limit:

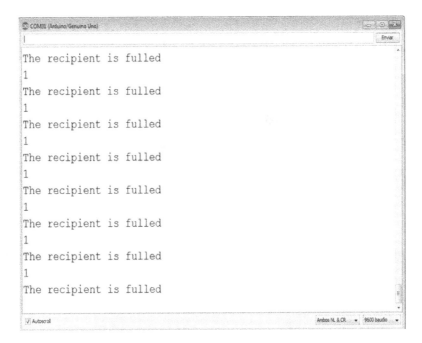

Measuring temperature, humidity, and light and displaying data on an LCD

In this section, I will teach you how to monitor temperature, humidity, and light detection on an LCD screen.

Hardware and software requirements

In this project, you will use an Arduino UNO board; but you can also use an Arduino MEGA, which also works perfectly.

For temperature reading, we require a DHT11 sensor, a resistor of 4.7k, a photoresistor (light sensor), and a 10k resistor.

It also requires a 16 x 2 LCD screen, where you performed the tests; I used an I2C communication module for the screen interfaced with Arduino card. I recommend using this communication since only two pins of Arduino are required for sending data:

Finally, it requires a breadboard and male-male and female-male cables for connections.

Here is the list of components for the project:

- Arduino UNO
- Temperature and humidity sensor DHT11
- LCD Screen 16 x 2
- Module I2C for LCD
- A breadboard
- Cables

We connect the different components:

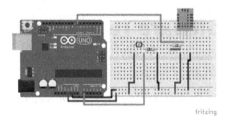

Here, we can see the image of the temperature and humidityDHT11 sensor:

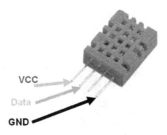

Then connect the pin number **1** of the **DHT11 sensor (VCC)** sensor to the red line on the breadboard and pin **4** (GND) to the blue line. Also, connect pin number **2** of the sensor to pin number **7** of the Arduino board. To end the DHT11 sensor, connect the resistance of 4.7k Ohms between pin number **1** and **2** of the sensor.

Place in series with the 10k Ohm resistance in the breadboard. Then connect the other end of the photoresistor to red on the breadboard and the other end of the resistance to the blue line (ground). Finally, connect the common pin between the photoresistor and resistance to the Arduino analog pin **A0**.

Now let's connect the LCD screen. Since we are using an LCD screen with an I2C interface, there are only two cables needed to connect to the signal and two for energy. Connect the pin of the I2C module called **VDC** to the red line on the breadboard and **GND** pin to the blue line on the breadboard. Then connect the **SDA** pin module to Arduino pin **A4,** and **A5 SCL** pin to pin the Arduino:

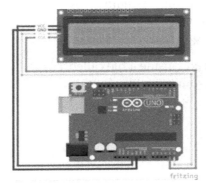

Here is an image of the project, fully assembled, so you can have an idea as to what the whole project will be:

Testing sensors

Now that the hardware project is fully assembled, we will test the different sensors. To do this, we will write a simple sketch in Arduino. We're just going to read the sensor data and print these data on the serial port.

You can now either copy the code inside a file called `Testing_sensors_Temp_Hum.ino`, or just get the complete code from the folder for this project.

First we define the libraries:

```
#include "DHT.h"
#define DHTPIN 7
#define DHTTYPE DHT11
```

We define the type of sensor:

```
DHT dht(DHTPIN, DHTTYPE);
```

Then we configure the serial communication:

```
void setup()
{
Serial.begin(9600);
dht.begin();
}
```

We read the sensor values:

```
void loop()
{
  float temp = dht.readTemperature();
  float hum = dht.readHumidity();
  float sensor = analogRead(0);
  float light = sensor / 1024 * 100;
```

We display the values on the serial interface:

```
  Serial.print("Temperature: ");
  Serial.print(temp);
  Serial.println(" C");
  Serial.print("Humidity: ");
  Serial.print(hum);
  Serial.println("%");
  Serial.print("Light: ");
  Serial.print(light);
  Serial.println("%");
  delay(700);
}
```

Download the code onto the Arduino board, and open the serial monitor to display the data sent. It is important to check the transmission speed serial port, which must be to 9600. Here is what you should see:

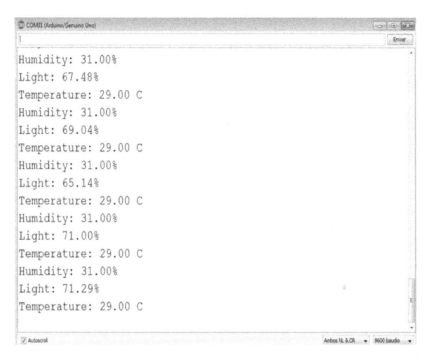

Displaying data on the LCD

Now the next step is to integrate our information to display on the LCD screen. The portion of sensor readings will be the same, only detailed with regard to communication and to display data on the LCD. The following is the complete code for this part, together with an explained.

You can now either copy the code inside a file called `LCD_sensors_temp_hum.ino`, or just get the complete code from the folder for this project.

We include the libraries for the program:

```
#include <Wire.h>
#include <LiquidCrystal_I2C.h>
#include "DHT.h"
#define DHTPIN 7
#define DHTTYPE DHT11
```

We define the LCD address for the LCD:

```
LiquidCrystal_I2C lcd(0x3F,16,2);
DHT dht(DHTPIN, DHTTYPE);
```

We start the LCD screen:

```
void setup()
{
lcd.init();
lcd.backlight();
lcd.setCursor(1,0);
lcd.print("Hello !!!");
lcd.setCursor(1,1);
lcd.print("Starting ...");
```

We define the beginning of the dht sensor:

```
dht.begin();
delay(2000);
lcd.clear();
}
```

We read the sensor and save the values in the variables:

```
void loop()
{
  float temp = dht.readTemperature();
  float hum = dht.readHumidity();
  float sensor = analogRead(0);
  float light = sensor / 1024 * 100;
```

We display the values on the LCD screen:

```
  lcd.setCursor(0,0);
  lcd.print("Temp:");
  lcd.print(temp,1);
  lcd.print((char)223);
  lcd.print("C");
  lcd.setCursor(0,1);
  lcd.print("Hum:");
  lcd.print(hum);
  lcd.print("%");
  lcd.setCursor(11,1);
  //lcd.print("L:");
  lcd.print(light);
  lcd.print("%");
  delay(700);
}
```

The next step is to download the example on the Arduino board; wait a little bit, and you will get display readings on the LCD. Here is an image of the project in action:

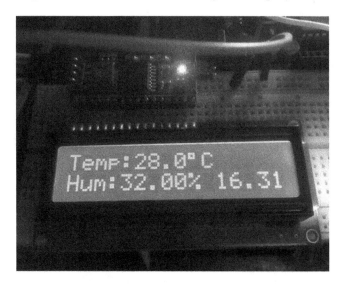

Detecting motion with a PIR sensor

We will build a project with a common home automation sensor: a motion sensor (PIR). Have you ever noticed those little white plastic modules that are in the top corners in some rooms of the houses, the modules that change color to red when someone walks in front of them? That's exactly what we will do in this project.

The motion sensor must have three pins: two for the power supply and one for the signal. You should also use a 5V voltage level to be compatible with the Arduino card, which also operates at 5V. The following image shows a simple motion sensor:

For practical purposes, we will use the signal input 8 for connecting the motion sensor, the signal voltage of 5 volts and ground **GND**.

PIR sensor interfaced with Arduino

PIR sensors detect body heat (infrared energy). Passive infrared sensors are the most widely used motion detectors in home security systems. Once the sensor warms up, it can detect heat and movement in the surrounding areas, creating a protective grid. If a moving object blocks too many grid zones and the infrared energy levels change rapidly, the sensors are tripped.

At this point, we will test the communication between the Arduino and the motion sensor.

We define the variable and the serial communication, define digital pin 8, input signal, read the state of the signal, and display the status signal of the sensor:

```
int sensor = 8;
void setup() {
Serial.begin(9600);
pinMode(sensor, INPUT);
}
void loop(){
// Readind the sensor
int state = digitalRead(sensor);
Serial.print("Detecting sensor: ");
Serial.println(state);
delay(100);
}
```

Detecting if the door is open with a reed switch

An example has been added as an option to implement a magnetic sensor in order to detect when a door or window is open or closed.

The sensor outputs a 0 when it detects the magnetic field and when the field is far away the output would be a 1; so you can determine when the door is open or closed.

The program in the Arduino is performed as follows:

We define the input signal of the sensor, and configure the serial communication:

```
void setup() {
  pinMode(sensor, INPUT_PULLUP);
  Serial.begin(9600);
}
```

We read the state of the sensor:

```
void loop() {
state = digitalRead(sensor);
```

It compares the digital input and displays the status of the door in the serial interface:

```
if (state == LOW){
   Serial.println("Door Close");
}
if (state == HIGH){
   Serial.println("Door Open");
}
}
```

Detecting who can get in the house with a fingerprint sensor

In this section, we will create a project that can help us make a complete security system. In this project, the fingerprint access will be addressed by reading the fingerprint using a fingerprint sensor as shown in the following image:

In this part, we will see how to connect and configure our hardware in order to activate our relay.

Hardware configuration:

As usual, we will use an Arduino Uno board as the brain of the project. The most important part of this project is the fingerprint sensor.

We are first going to see how to assemble the different parts of this project. Let's start by connecting the power supply. Connect the **5V** pin from the Arduino board to the red power rail and the **GND** from Arduino to the blue power rail on the breadboard.

Now, let's connect the fingerprint sensor. First, connect the power by connecting the cables to their respective color on the breadboard. Then, connect the white wire from the sensor to Arduino pin 3 and the green wire to pin number 2.

After that, we are going to connect the relay module. Connect the **VCC** pin to the red power rail, **GND** pin to the blue power rail, and the **EN** pin to Arduino pin 7:

Save the fingerprint:

The following example is presented to register the ID's fingerprints directly from the library `Adafruit_Fingerprint`.

Firstly, we define the libraries:

```
#include <Adafruit_Fingerprint.h>
#include <SoftwareSerial.h>
```

We define the ID of the reading and the function of the enroll process:

```
uint8_t id;
uint8_tgetFingerprintEnroll();
```

We define the serial communication with the device:

```
SoftwareSerialmySerial(2, 3);
Adafruit_Fingerprint finger = Adafruit_Fingerprint(&mySerial);
```

We declare the instance of the sensor:

```
//Adafruit_Fingerprint finger = Adafruit_Fingerprint(&Serial1);
```

We set up and display if the sensor is being configured:

```
void setup()
{
  while (!Serial);
  delay(500);
```

We display the sensor confirmation:

```
Serial.begin(9600);
Serial.println("Adafruit Fingerprint sensor enrollment");
// set the data rate for the sensor serial port
finger.begin(57600);
```

We identify the sensor if it detects:

```
if (finger.verifyPassword()) {
Serial.println("Found fingerprint sensor!");
} else {
  Serial.println("Did not find fingerprint sensor :(");
  while (1);
  }
}
uint8_treadnumber(void) {
uint8_tnum = 0;
booleanvalidnum = false;
while (1) {
  while (! Serial.available());
    char c = Serial.read();
    if (isdigit(c)) {
      num *= 10;
      num += c - '0';
      validnum = true;
      } else if (validnum) {
        returnnum;
```

```
        }
      }
    }
```

We display the enrolling ID:

```
void loop()                        // run over and over again
{
Serial.println("Ready to enroll a fingerprint! Please Type in the ID # you
want to save this finger as...");
id = readnumber();
Serial.print("Enrolling ID #");
Serial.println(id);

while (!  getFingerprintEnroll() );
}
```

The function for enrolling is as follows:

```
uint8_tgetFingerprintEnroll() {
int p = -1;
Serial.print("Waiting for valid finger to enroll as #");
Serial.println(id);
while (p != FINGERPRINT_OK) {
    p = finger.getImage();
switch (p) {
case FINGERPRINT_OK:
Serial.println("Image taken");
break;
case FINGERPRINT_NOFINGER:
Serial.println(".");
break;
case FINGERPRINT_PACKETRECIEVEERR:
Serial.println("Communication error");
break;
case FINGERPRINT_IMAGEFAIL:
Serial.println("Imaging error");
break;
default:
Serial.println("Unknown error");
break;
    }
  }
```

If the sensor successfully reads the image you see the following:

```
    p = finger.image2Tz(1);
switch (p) {
case FINGERPRINT_OK:
Serial.println("Image converted");
break;
case FINGERPRINT_IMAGEMESS:
Serial.println("Image too messy");
return p;
case FINGERPRINT_PACKETRECIEVEERR:
Serial.println("Communication error");
return p;
case FINGERPRINT_FEATUREFAIL:
Serial.println("Could not find fingerprint features");
return p;
case FINGERPRINT_INVALIDIMAGE:
```

If it cannot find the fingerprint features, you see the following:Serial.println("Could not find fingerprint features");

```
return p;
default:
Serial.println("Unknown error");
return p;
    }
```

Remove the fingerprint sensor:

```
Serial.println("Remove finger");
delay(2000);
    p = 0;
while (p != FINGERPRINT_NOFINGER) {
p = finger.getImage();
    }
Serial.print("ID "); Serial.println(id);
p = -1;
Serial.println("Place same finger again");
while (p != FINGERPRINT_OK) {
    p = finger.getImage();
switch (p) {
case FINGERPRINT_OK:
Serial.println("Image taken");
break;
case FINGERPRINT_NOFINGER:
Serial.print(".");
break;
case FINGERPRINT_PACKETRECIEVEERR:
```

```
Serial.println("Communication error");
break;
case FINGERPRINT_IMAGEFAIL:
Serial.println("Imaging error");
break;
default:
Serial.println("Unknown error");
break;
    }
  }
```

Image for the fingerprint sensor:

```
  p = finger.image2Tz(2);
switch (p) {
case FINGERPRINT_OK:
Serial.println("Image converted");
break;
case FINGERPRINT_IMAGEMESS:
Serial.println("Image too messy");
return p;
case FINGERPRINT_PACKETRECIEVEERR:
Serial.println("Communication error");
return p;
case FINGERPRINT_FEATUREFAIL:
Serial.println("Could not find fingerprint features");
return p;
case FINGERPRINT_INVALIDIMAGE:
Serial.println("Could not find fingerprint features");
return p;
default:
Serial.println("Unknown error");
return p;
    }
```

If it is correct, you see the following:

```
Serial.print("Creating model for #");  Serial.println(id);

  p = finger.createModel();
if (p == FINGERPRINT_OK) {
Serial.println("Prints matched!");
  } else if (p == FINGERPRINT_PACKETRECIEVEERR) {
Serial.println("Communication error");
return p;
  } else if (p == FINGERPRINT_ENROLLMISMATCH) {
Serial.println("Fingerprints did not match");
return p;
  } else {
Serial.println("Unknown error");
return p;
  }
```

Display the result of the sensor:

```
Serial.print("ID "); Serial.println(id);
  p = finger.storeModel(id);
if (p == FINGERPRINT_OK) {
Serial.println("Stored!");
  } else if (p == FINGERPRINT_PACKETRECIEVEERR) {
Serial.println("Communication error");
return p;
  } else if (p == FINGERPRINT_BADLOCATION) {
Serial.println("Could not store in that location");
return p;
  } else if (p == FINGERPRINT_FLASHERR) {
Serial.println("Error writing to flash");
return p;
  } else {
Serial.println("Unknown error");
return p;
}
}
```

Testing the sensor

Open the serial monitor, then type the ID number saved in the previous step:

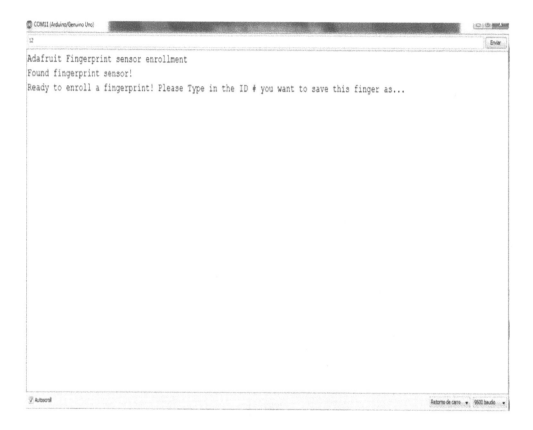

The following screenshot indicates that you should put the same finger on the sensor again:

The following screenshot shows that the sensor responses indicates that the digital fingerprint has been successfully saved:

Summary

In this chapter, we saw how to interact with different sensors connected to the Arduino board, such as flow current for energy consumption, detecting a risk in the home, implementing a gas sensor, implementing flow water sensor to measure the water volume, making a security system, and controlling access with a fingerprint sensor. All of these sensors can be integrate a complete system for monitoring and controlling everything you work on any project.

In the next chapter, we will see how to integrate everything for monitoring and controlling a complete system, and reading the sensors and actuators in a dashboard using your Arduino board and the Raspberry Pi Zero as a central interface.

4
Control-Connected Devices

In this chapter, we will look at how to control devices from remote sites using our Raspberry Pi Zero and Arduino UNO, using the following modules to communicate in a network: Wi-Fi shield and Ethernet shield. We will cover the following topics in this chapter:

- Making a simple web server with Node.js
- Controlling a relay from a Raspberry Pi Zero using Restful API and Node.js
- Configuring Node.js in a computer as a web server
- Monitoring temperature, humidity, and light using Node.js with Arduino Wi-Fi
- Monitoring temperature, humidity, and light using Node.js with Arduino Ethernet

Making a simple web server with Node.js

One of the most important aspect of having a Raspberry Pi is that we have a real computer configured with services and servers. In this section, we will explain how to install Node.js, which is a powerful framework that we will use to run most of the applications we are going to see in this book. Luckily for us, installing Node.js on Raspberry Pi is really simple.

In the folder for this chapter, open the file called `webserver.js`. We will create a server on port *8056*. To test the program and see the results we have to open the Node.js terminal on your MS-DOS interface and run this file with the following command:

```
node webserver.js
```

Add the following lines to `webserver.js` file to declare the HTTP request commands:

```
var http = require('http');
```

We create the server with the following function:

```
http.createServer(function (req, res) {
```

We define the content of the file that we will show in the HTML code:

```
res.writeHead(200, {'Content-Type': 'text/plain'});
```

We send the response from the server:

```
res.end('Hello  from Node.js');
```

It's important to define the port that is going to be opened:

```
}).listen(8056);
```

Display the message of the server:

```
console.log('Server running at port 8056');
```

To test this program, open the browser on your local computer and navigate to the following link: `http://192.168.1.105:8056`. If you see the following screen; your Node.js server is running perfectly on your computer; you need to change the IP address of your computer:

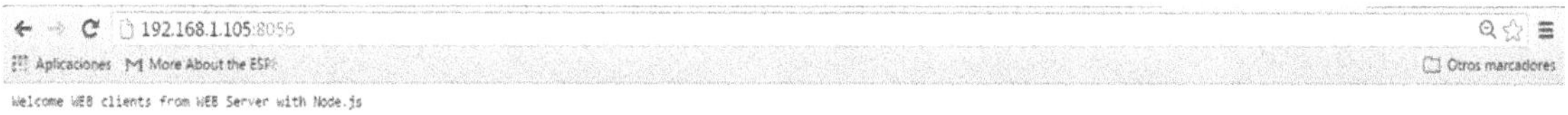

Controlling a relay from a Raspberry Pi Zero using Restful API and Node.js

In this section, we will show you how to control a relay module connected to an Arduino UNO board, a relay for sending commands from a web browser. Let's do it.

JSON structure

JavaScript Object Notation (JSON) is a lightweight data-interchange format. It is easy for humans to read and write. It is easy for machines to parse and generate. It is based on a subset of the JavaScript Programming Language.

JSON is built on two structures:

- A collection of name/value pairs. In various languages, this is realized as an object, record, struct, dictionary, hash table, keyed list, or associative array.

- An ordered list of values. In most languages, this is realized as an array, vector, list, or sequence.

First, we need to know how to apply the JSON format that we use to describe this structure, as follows:

```
{"data": "Pin D6 set to 1", "id": "1", "name": "Arduino", "connected":
true}
```

This is the format that we need to follow and make responsive:

- **Data:** Defines the number of the command and then describes the definition of the command
- **Name:** Follows the name of the device
- **Connected:** Confirms if the device is connected or not

All the data that is between the { } defines our JSON format.

Commands with the aREST API

Using the aREST command like this, we can define our Arduino and the devices, and then control them from a web browser. The following are examples of the commands from the aREST API:

- IP_Address_of the device/mode/6/o: This configures the digital pin 6 like an output pin
- IP_Address_of the device /digital/6/1: Configures output 6 and makes the function like a digitalwrite. For example: http://192.168.1.100/digital/6/1; we define the IP address of the device and the number of the pin that will be activated.

Installing Node.js on your Raspberry Pi Zero

Node.js is a tool that will allow us to create servers running in the device, using code in JavaScript. The most important thing is that we will apply this framework to build a web server using this code.

Using Node.js means that we configure a web server that will open a port and the devices can be connected to the web server.

With the following command, you will install Node.js in your Raspberry Pi Zero:

```
sudo apt-get install nodejs
```

NPM is the default package manager for the JavaScript runtime environment with Node.js. To configure and install the aREST module, type the following line in your terminal:

```
sudo npm install arest
```

The Express philosophy is to provide small, robust tooling for HTTP servers, making it a great solution for single-page applications, websites, hybrids, or public HTTP APIs.

We can also need to configure the express module with the following command:

```
sudo npm install express
```

Controlling the relay using aREST commands from a web browser

In the next section, we will see how to control a digital output from a web browser using Rest commands. Let's dive into it, to see more details:

Configuring the web server

You can now either copy the code inside a file called outputcontrol.js, or just get the complete code from the folder for this project and execute it with Node.js. Open the terminal on your Raspberry Pi and type the following:

```
sudo node output control.js
```

We define the GPIO of the device importing the commands, by using the following:

```
var gpio = require('rpi-gpio');
```

Now we will create our web server using Node.js using the following lines.

We import the require packages that are necessary to run. We declare the libraries using the following:

```
var express = require('express');
var app = express();
```

Define the body parser and open the port, in this case, *8099*:

```
var Parser = require('body-parser');
var port = 8099;
```

Use the body-parser:

```
app.use(Parser.urlencoded({ extended: false }));
app.use(Parser.json());
```

Configure **GPIO 11**, which we will control:

```
gpio.setup(11, gpio.DIR_OUT);
```

We define the functions that we will call from the web browser.

The name of the function is `ledon`; it activates the **GPIO 11** and sends the message `led1 is on` to the screen:

```
function ledon() {
    setTimeout(function() {
        console.log('led1 is on');
        gpio.write(11, 1);
    }, 2000);
}
```

The name of the function is `ledoff`; it turns off the **GPIO 11** and sends the message `led1 is off` to the screen:

```
function ledoff() {
    setTimeout(function() {
        console.log('led1 is off');
        gpio.write(11, 0);
    }, 2000);
}
```

We define the function `GET`, which means that we are making a request to the server when the browser receives the function called `ledon`; it responds with following format: `{status:"connected",led:"on"}`.

We will now declare the app function for the incoming requests from the clients:

```
app.get('/ledon', function (req, res) {
    ledon();
    var data ={status:"connected",led:"on"};
    res.json(data);
});
```

We define the function `GET` .which means that we are making a request to the server when the browser receives the function called `/ledoff`, it responds with following format: `{status:"connected",led:"off"}`.

```
app.get('/ledoff', function (req, res) {
    ledoff();
    var data ={status:"connected",led:"off"};
    res.json(data);
});
```

We now open the port from the web server:

```
app.listen(port);
console.log('Server was started on ' + port);
```

If everything is correct, we open our favorite browser and type `http://IP_address of your Raspberry_PI_zero:port/command`.

In this case, we type `192.168.1.105:8099/ledon`.

The following screenshot shows you the response of the JSON request:

After that, we will see the final result, as shown in the following image:

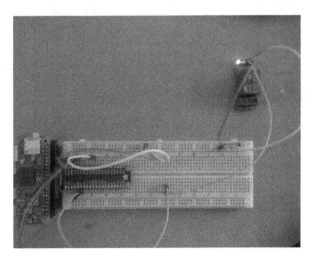

Configuring Node.js on a computer as a web server

Node.js is an open-source, cross-platform runtime environment for developing server-side and networking applications. Node.js applications are written in JavaScript, and can be run within the Node.js runtime on OS X, Microsoft Windows, and Linux.

Node.js also provides a rich library of various JavaScript modules that simplify the development of web applications using Node.js to a great extent.

In the last section, we configured Node.js in Raspberry Pi Zero, now in this section we will do the same thing using a Windows operating system and configure our web server Node.js running on it.

The main purpose of this section is to explain how to control our Arduino boards from a web server running in the Node.js framework. For that, it's important to install it; our system will run on Windows computer.

In this section, we will explain how to install Node.js in Windows.

Downloading Node.js

First we need to download Node.js for Windows 64 bit – it depends of the version of your operating system to download it, you just need to go to the following link: `https://nodejs.org/es/download/`:

Installing Node.js

After we have downloaded the software, follow these steps:

1. Click on the **Next** button:

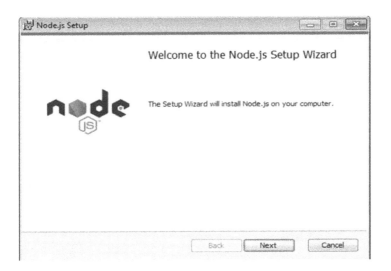

2. Click on the **Next** button:

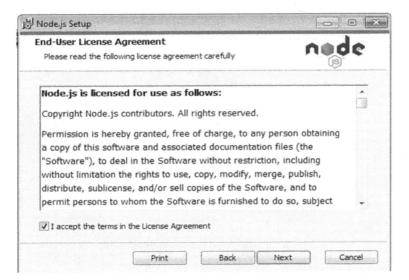

3. Select where to install it:

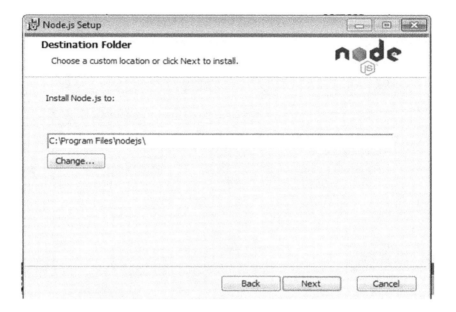

4. Select the default configuration:

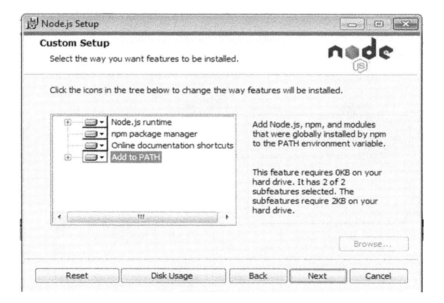

5. To finish the configuration, we click on **Install**:

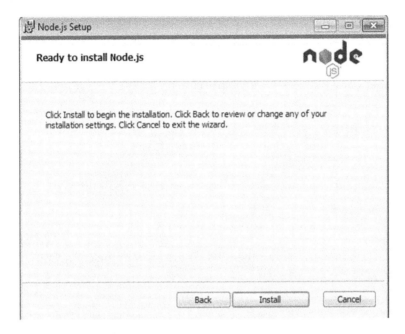

6. After the installation is complete we will see the following:

Configuring web server port 8080 with Node.js

Now we need to configure the port that will be expected to listen to the opening connection from the remote browsers. Open the file that is in the folder of this chapter, and then execute the file with Node.js.

You can now either copy the code inside a file called `server.js`, or just get the complete code from the folder for this project.

First we need to create our server with the following code:

```
var server = require('http');
```

Create a function named `loadServer` that has the code to respond to the browser:

```
function loadServer(requiere,response){
        console.log("Somebody is connected");
```

If this function responds with the number 200 , it means that the connection is established, the server works perfectly:

```
response.writeHead(200,{"Content-Type":"text/html"});
        response.write("<h1>The Server works perfect</h1>");
        response.end();
}
```

Create and open the server port:

```
server.createServer(loadServer).listen(8080);
```

Open the Terminal with the Node.js server installed on your computer, and then in your MS-DOS interface, type the following command:

```
C:\users\PC>node server.js
```

Now, to test weather the server is running, we will go the web browser and type `localhost:number_of_port;` and you should see on your screen similar to the following screenshot:

```
http://localhost:8080
```

The Server works perfect

Monitoring temperature, humidity, and light using Node.js with Arduino Wi-Fi

In this part of the chapter, we will explain the code for the Wi-Fi shield with Arduino:

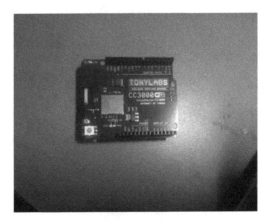

We define the number of variables; in this case we will monitor three variables (`temperature`, `humidity`, and `light`):

```
#define NUMBER_VARIABLES 3
```

Here we have to include the library for the sensor:

```
#include "DHT.h"
```

We define the pin for the sensor:

```
#define DHTPIN 7
#define DHTTYPE DHT11
```

We define the instance of the sensor:

```
DHT dht(DHTPIN, DHTTYPE);
```

We import the libraries for the module:

```
#include <Adafruit_CC3000.h>
#include <SPI.h>
#include <CC3000_MDNS.h>
#include <aREST.h>
```

We define the pins for connecting the module:

```
using a breakout board
#define ADAFRUIT_CC3000_IRQ    3
#define ADAFRUIT_CC3000_VBAT   5
#define ADAFRUIT_CC3000_CS     10
```

We create the instance of the module that will be connected:

```
Adafruit_CC3000 cc3000 = Adafruit_CC3000(ADAFRUIT_CC3000_CS,
ADAFRUIT_CC3000_IRQ, ADAFRUIT_CC3000_VBAT);
```

We define the aREST instance:

```
aREST rest = aREST();
```

Then we define the SSID and password, which you need to change:

```
#define WLAN_SSID        "xxxxx"
#define WLAN_PASS        "xxxxx"
#define WLAN_SECURITY    WLAN_SEC_WPA2
```

We configure the port to listen for incoming TCP connections:

```
#define LISTEN_PORT          80
```

We define the server instance of the module:

```
Adafruit_CC3000_Server restServer(LISTEN_PORT);
// DNS responder instance
MDNSResponder mdns;
```

We define the variables that will be published:

```
int temp;
int hum;
int light;
```

We have here the setup that defines the configuration of serial communications:

```
void setup(void)
{
  // Start Serial
  Serial.begin(115200);
  dht.begin();
```

We begin the variables that will be published:

```
rest.variable("light",&light);
rest.variable("temp",&temp);
rest.variable("hum",&hum);
```

We define the ID and the name of the device:

```
rest.set_id("001");
rest.set_name("monitor");
```

We connect to the network:

```
if (!cc3000.begin())
{
  while(1);
}
if (!cc3000.connectToAP(WLAN_SSID, WLAN_PASS, WLAN_SECURITY)) {
  while(1);
}
while (!cc3000.checkDHCP())
{
  delay(100);
}
```

Here we define the function to get the device connected:

```
if (!mdns.begin("arduino", cc3000)) {
  while(1);
}
```

We display the connections in the serial interface:

```
displayConnectionDetails();
restServer.begin();
Serial.println(F("Listening for connections..."));
}
```

In this part, we declare the variables that will be acquired:

```
void loop() {
  temp = (float)dht.readTemperature();
  hum = (float)dht.readHumidity();
```

We then measure light level:

```
float sensor_reading = analogRead(A0);
light = (int)(sensor_reading/1024*100);
```

We declare the function for requesting:

```
mdns.update();
```

We need to execute the requests from the server:

```
Adafruit_CC3000_ClientRef client = restServer.available();
rest.handle(client);
}
```

We display the networking configuration from the device:

```
bool displayConnectionDetails(void)
{
  uint32_t ipAddress, netmask, gateway, dhcpserv, dnsserv;
  if(!cc3000.getIPAddress(&ipAddress, &netmask, &gateway, &dhcpserv,
&dnsserv))
  {
Serial.println(F("Unable to retrieve the IP Address!\r\n"));
    return false;
  }
  else
  {
    Serial.print(F("\nIP Addr: ")); cc3000.printIPdotsRev(ipAddress);
    Serial.print(F("\nNetmask: ")); cc3000.printIPdotsRev(netmask);
```

```
    Serial.print(F("\nGateway: ")); cc3000.printIPdotsRev(gateway);
    Serial.print(F("\nDHCPsrv: ")); cc3000.printIPdotsRev(dhcpserv);
    Serial.print(F("\nDNSserv: ")); cc3000.printIPdotsRev(dnsserv);
    Serial.println();
    return true;
  }
}
```

Download the sketch of code in your Arduino board, and then go to the serial monitor to see the configuration of the IP address taken from your router. After that, we can display the configuration IP address of the Wi-Fi shield:

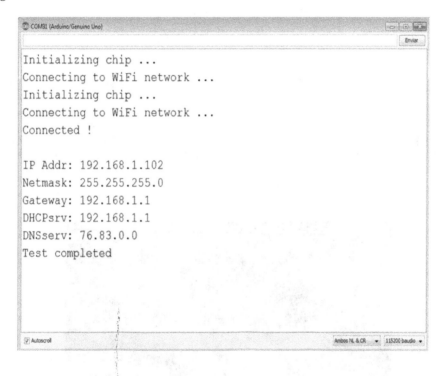

Connecting to the Wi-Fi network

Now that we can see the IP address of your Arduino Wi-Fi shield, we can now connect our computer to the same network as the Arduino board. Look at the following screenshot to see more details:

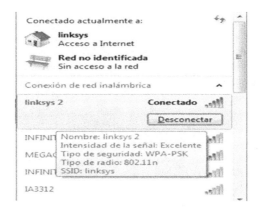

To test the application, we need to go to the following path and run the following commands on the computer that you have installed your Node.js server, on as shown in the following screenshot:

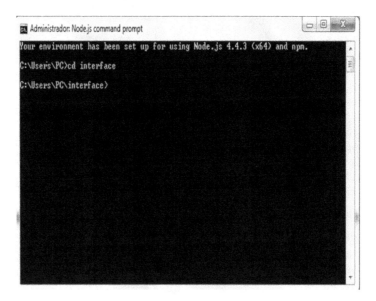

In this folder, we have the file in JavaScript and type the command node app.js

After entering the interface folder type the following command `node app.js`:

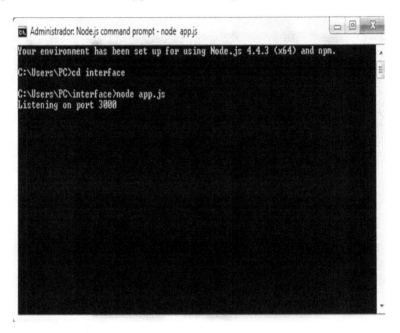

Now that you have launched the web server, application, switch over to a browser, on the same machine to see the results by entering the IP address of the machine:

After the server is listening on port 300, it establishes communication with the Wi-Fi module sending a request to the IP address of the device:

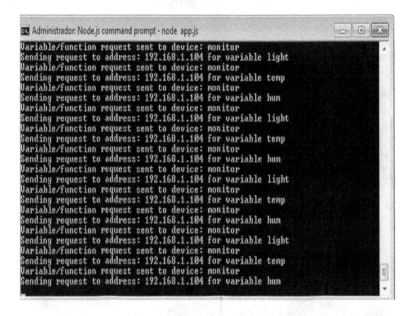

Monitoring temperature, humidity, and light using Node.js with Arduino Ethernet

In the preceding section, we showed how to monitor our Arduino via Wi-Fi using the *CC3000* module; now we will use another important module: Ethernet Shield. The hardware connection of the part is similar to the following image:

Code for the application of the Arduino Ethernet shield

You can now either copy the code inside a file called `Monitor_Ethernet.ino`, or just get the complete code from the folder for this project; you need to use the Arduino IDE.

The following are the libraries included in the program:

```
#include <SPI.h>
#include <Ethernet.h>
#include <aREST.h>
#include <avr/wdt.h>
```

Include the library for the DHT11 sensor:

```
#include "DHT.h"
```

We define the pins for the temperature and humidity sensor:

```
#define DHTPIN 7
#define DHTTYPE DHT11
```

We have the instance of the sensor:

```
DHT dht(DHTPIN, DHTTYPE);
```

We register the MAC address for the device:

```
byte mac[] = { 0x90, 0xA2, 0xDA, 0x0E, 0xFE, 0x40 };
IPAddress ip(192,168,1,153);
EthernetServer server(80);
```

We now create an instance of the aREST API:

```
aREST rest = aREST();
```

We publish the variables that will be monitored:

```
int temp;
int hum;
int light;
```

We now configure serial communication and start the instance of the sensor:

```
void setup(void)
{
  // Start Serial
  Serial.begin(115200);
  dht.begin();
```

We start the variables to publish:

```
  rest.variable("light",&light);
  rest.variable("temp",&temp);
  rest.variable("hum",&hum);
```

It is very important to give the ID and the name of the device that we are using:

```
  rest.set_id("008");
  rest.set_name("Ethernet");
```

We begin the Ethernet connection:

```
if (Ethernet.begin(mac) == 0) {
    Serial.println("Failed to configure Ethernet using DHCP");
    Ethernet.begin(mac, ip);
  }
```

We display the IP address on the serial monitor:

```
  server.begin();
  Serial.print("server is at ");
  Serial.println(Ethernet.localIP());
  wdt_enable(WDTO_4S);
}
```

We read the temperature and humidity sensor:

```
void loop() {

  temp = (float)dht.readTemperature();
  hum = (float)dht.readHumidity();
```

We measure the light level of the sensor:

```
  float sensor_reading = analogRead(A0);
  light = (sensor_reading/1024*100);
```

We listen for the incoming clients that will be connected:

```
EthernetClient client = server.available();
rest.handle(client);
wdt_reset();
}
```

Now that we have finished the configurations, we open a web browser and type the IP address of your Arduino Ethernet shield: `http://192.168.1.153`. If everything goes perfectly it will display the following screen with the JSON response from the board:

The preceding screenshot shows the results of the JSON request.

Configuring the device in Node.js

In this section, we will explain the code for configuring the devices that we can control from a web page.

We installed the express package in the previous section; if you have any difficulty, just open a terminal and type the following:

```
npm install express
```

We define the node express and create the app:

```
var express = require('express');
var app = express();
```

We then define the port to listen:

```
var port = 3000;
```

We define the instance of Jade application, using the view engine:

```
app.set('view engine', 'jade');
```

We configure the public folder:

```
app.use(express.static(__dirname + '/public'));
```

We now define the devices to monitor:

```
var rest = require("arest")(app);
rest.addDevice('http','192.168.1.153');
```

We serve the application:

```
app.get('/', function(req, res){
res.render('interface');
});
```

We start the server and send the message when the device is connected:

```
app.listen(port);
console.log("Listening on port " + port);
```

Open your terminal in MS-DOS and execute app.js in your Node.js server

To test the application, open your web browser and type http://localhost:3000; if a screen like the following, congratulations appears, you just configured your server properly:

Here we have the screen where we see the execution of `app.js` in the Node.js server:

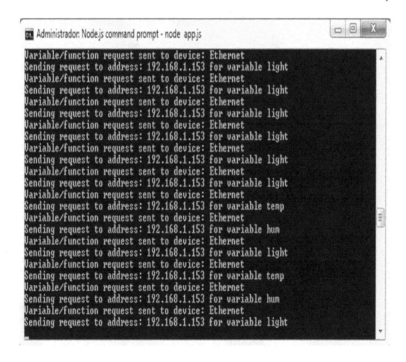

Summary

In this chapter, you learned how to control your Arduino board, using modules of communication in a networking area from the Raspberry Pi Zero in a central interface Dashboard. We have looked at how to control and monitor devices from a central interface; you can use other sensors, for example, a sensor barometric pressure.

In the next chapter, you will do more interesting projects such as configuring and connecting a web camera to your Arduino board that can be monitored from your Raspberry Pi Zero.

5
Adding a Webcam to Monitor Your Security System

In the previous chapters, we talked about topics such as sensors connected to the Arduino and monitoring from the Raspberry Pi Zero, using a network across devices, the importance of our home security projects, and domotics to monitor what's happening in the real world. For that, we have a proposal for this chapter.

In this chapter, we will configure our Raspberry Pi Zero to monitor a web camera and install a TTL serial camera to interact with Arduino boards; we will achieve that with the following topics:

- Interaction between Arduino and Raspberry Pi
- Controlling an output connected to Arduino from Raspberry Pi Zero
- Connecting a TTL serial camera to Arduino and saving pictures to a Micro SD
- Detecting motion with the serial TTL camera
- Controlling a snapshot from Raspberry Pi
- Controlling your camera from a web page
- Monitoring your USB camera for security in a network

Interaction between Arduino and Raspberry Pi

In this chapter, we will look at how the Raspberry Pi can work as a terminal computer to program, not only having the device as a server and deploying pages or applications but also have an IDE for programming the Arduino board. To do this we need to have the Raspberry Pi connected to the Arduino, so that they can communicate with each other.

Here are some interfaces that the Raspberry Pi has, all of these which included in the device: I2C protocol, SPI communication, USB ports, and serial **UART** ports. In this case, we will use the USB port to communicate between Arduino and the Raspberry Pi.

These are the steps to configure Arduino and Raspberry Pi to interact with each other:

1. Install Arduino IDE for the Raspberry Pi
2. Open your terminal with PuTTY and check the IP address of your Raspberry Pi
3. Execute remote access, and type the IP address
4. Open Arduino IDE in the graphical interface

Installing Arduino IDE in Raspbian

Type the following command to install Arduino IDE on the Raspberry Pi:

```
sudo apt-get install arduino
```

Remote access to Raspberry Pi

In this section, we will look at the screen to access the Remote desk to execute the Arduino IDE installed in the Raspian operating system: once the screen pops up, type your username and password:

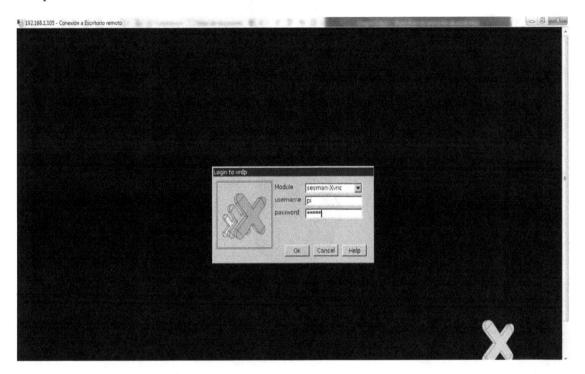

Executing Arduino in a graphical interface

Now that we have the main screen, we go to the **Programming** menu, and if we see the icon to enter the Arduino IDE, everything is installed. Click on the icon of the **Arduino IDE**:

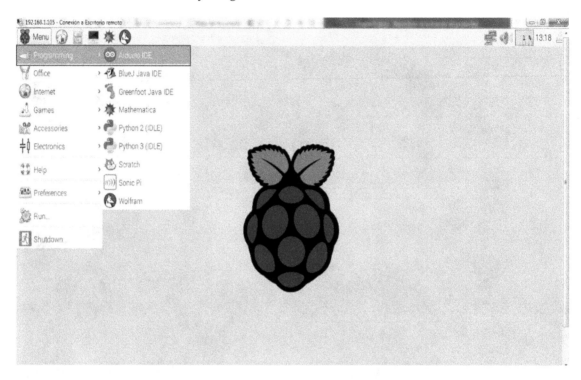

Arduino interface in Raspian

Here we have the interface of the Arduino IDE, similar to the ones we have in a computer. From the Arduino IDE running in the Raspberry Pi, we can interact between both boards:

Preparing the interface

We need to verify that we selected the proper board; in this case, we're using an Arduino UNO. Select the board in the following window:

Selecting the serial port

After we have selected the board that we will use, we need to verify and select the port that will communicate with our Arduino connected to the USB port of the Raspberry Pi; we need to select the name port: `/dev/ttyACM0`:

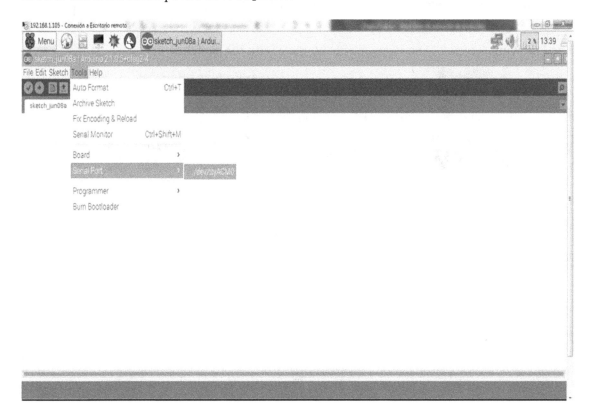

Downloading a sketch from the graphical interface

The main thing that we need is to communicate with Arduino from our Raspberry Pi Zero and download the sketch to the Arduino board without using a computer, so that we can use our Raspberry Pi for other purposes.

The following screenshot shows you the interface with the sketch:

We should download the sketch in the interface. The following image shows the connected Arduino-Raspberry Pi: that's cool!

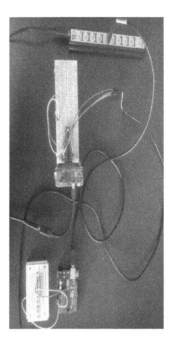

Controlling an output connected to Arduino from Raspberry Pi Zero

Now we will look at an example of controlling an output from the Raspberry Pi, using Python.

First we need to download the sketch to the Arduino board. To test our communication, we will show an example of testing the link between the Arduino and the Raspberry Pi:

We declare the following output:

```
int led_output = 13;
```

We start with the setup in the program:

```
void setup () {
```

Then we mention the output pin:

```
pinMode(led_output, OUTPUT);
```

Start the serial communication at 9600:

```
Serial.begin(9600);
}
```

Declare the loop of the program:

```
void loop () {
```

This is where we check weather serial port is available or not:

```
if (Serial.available() > 0){
```

If something found it reads something and saves the content in c variable:

```
char c = Serial.read();
```

If it reads a letter H which is marked for high:

```
if (c == 'H'){
```

The output will turn on the LED connected to pin **13**

```
digitalWrite(led_output, HIGH);
```

In case it reads a letter L which is marked for low:

```
}
else if (c == 'L'){
```

The output will turn off the LED connected to pin **13**:

```
digitalWrite(led_output, LOW);
}
}
}
```

Controlling the Arduino board from Python

First we need to install the serial library, as this helps to communicate with Arduino via the USB port communication. Type the following command to install the library:

```
sudo apt-get install python-serial
```

The following code controls Arduino from Raspberry Pi; you can now either copy the code inside a file called ControlArduinoFromRasp.py, or just get the complete code from the folder for this project.

The following snippet imports the serial library in Python:

```
import serial
```

We define the serial communication:

```
Arduino_UNO = serial.Serial('/dev/ttyACM0', 9600)
```

Print a message to see that the communication is done:

```
print("Hello From Arduino!")
```

While this executes, the user can enter a command:

```
while True:
        command = raw_input('Enter the command ')
        Arduino_UNO.write(command)
```

If it's an H it prints the message; in case it is false it displays LED off:

```
        if command == 'H':
                print('LED ON')
        elif command == 'L':
                print('LED OFF')
```

Close the connection:

```
arduino_UNO.close()
```

Hardware connections

This is the LED connected to Arduino UNO, and it can be controlled from the Raspberry Pi using Python:

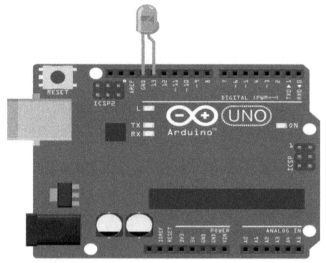

Made with **Fritzing.org**

Connecting a TTL serial camera to Arduino and saving pictures to a micro SD

Here we have the schema, with the connections of the micro SD card with the TTL serial camera; I use a camera model from Adafruit. The following link has all the information you need, https://www.adafruit.com/product/397. In the following image, we have the connections of the project:

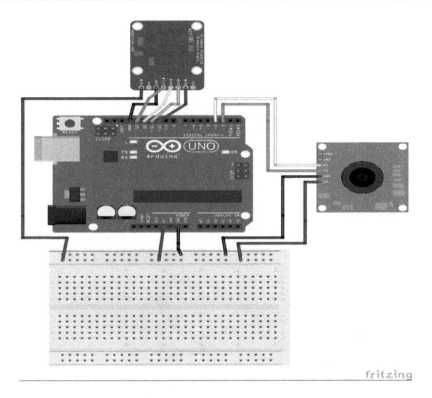

fritzing

Now we will explain how to take a picture and save it to a micro SD; the main idea is to connect a camera to the Arduino, so we can implement this in a system monitoring for home security.

The following is the code for testing the TTL camera, taking a picture, and saving it on a micro SD. Note that the code is too long, but I will be explaining the most important and necessary code to do the previous actions. All the code for these examples is included with the book for more complete information.

Here we have the import files from the TTL camera, and the files to communicate with the micro SD:

```
#include <Adafruit_VC0706.h>
#include <SPI.h>
#include <SD.h>
```

We define the library software to communicate via serial:

```
// comment out this line if using Arduino V23 or earlier
#include <SoftwareSerial.h>
```

define the `chipSelect` to pin 10:

```
#define chipSelect 10
```

The code will pin for connections:

```
SoftwareSerial cameraconnection = SoftwareSerial(2, 3);
Adafruit_VC0706 cam = Adafruit_VC0706(&cameraconnection);
```

Then we will need to start the camera:

```
if (cam.begin()) {
  Serial.println("Camera Found:");
} else {
  Serial.println("No camera found?");
  return;
}
```

Here we define the image size:

```
cam.setImageSize(VC0706_640x480);
```

This will display the image size:

```
uint8_t imgsize = cam.getImageSize();
Serial.print("Image size: ");
```

The code will take a picture:

```
if (! cam.takePicture())
  Serial.println("Failed to snap!");
else
  Serial.println("Picture taken!");
```

Create the file to save the image taken:

```
char filename[13];
```

Code to save the file:

```
strcpy(filename, "IMAGE00.JPG");
for (int i = 0; i < 100; i++) {
  filename[5] = '0' + i/10;
  filename[6] = '0' + i%10;
```

Prepare the micro SD to save the files:

```
if (! SD.exists(filename)) {
     break;
   }
 }
```

Open the file taken for prewview:

```
File imgFile = SD.open(filename, FILE_WRITE);
```

To show the size of the image taken:

```
uint16_t jpglen = cam.frameLength();
Serial.print("Storing ");
Serial.print(jpglen, DEC);
Serial.print(" byte image.");
```

Read the data from the file:

```
byte wCount = 0; // For counting # of writes
while (jpglen > 0) {
```

Write the file into the memory:

```
uint8_t *buffer;
uint8_t bytesToRead = min(32, jpglen);
buffer = cam.readPicture(bytesToRead);
imgFile.write(buffer, bytesToRead);
```

Display the file on the screen:

```
if(++wCount >= 64) {
   Serial.print('.');
   wCount = 0;
 }
```

Display the number of bytes read:

```
Serial.print(bytesToRead, DEC);
Serial.println(" bytes");
jpglen -= bytesToRead;
 }
```

Close the file which is open:

```
imgFile.close();
```

Detecting motion with the serial TTL camera

Turn on the motion detection of TTL camera:

```
cam.setMotionDetect(true);
```

Verify if the motion is activated:

```
Serial.print("Motion detection is ");
if (cam.getMotionDetect())
  Serial.println("ON");
else
  Serial.println("OFF");
}
```

What happens when motion is detected by the camera:

```
if (cam.motionDetected()) {
  Serial.println("Motion!");
  cam.setMotionDetect(false);
```

If motion is detected, take the picture or display the message:

```
if (! cam.takePicture())
  Serial.println("Failed to snap!");
else
  Serial.println("Picture taken!");
```

Controlling a snapshot from Raspberry Pi

Now that we have seen how to communicate between Arduino and Raspberry Pi, to control the board, we can apply this to our security system project. We need to do this for communicating with and controlling our camera from the Raspberry Pi:

- Connect the Arduino and Raspberry Pi to each other
- Create a serial connection at 9,600 mbps
- Call the function that will take the picture and save it in the micro SD

On the Raspberry Pi we need to do the following:

- Create the script for calling the function in the Arduino that will take the picture
- Open and execute the script using your PuTTY terminal

The following section is the sketch that should be download in the Arduino board:

First we start the serial communication:

```
void setup () {
    Serial.begin(9600);
}
```

This is the function that will tell the camera to take the picture:

```
void loop () {
    if (Serial.available() > 0) {
        char c = Serial.read();
        if (c == 'T') {
        takingpicture():


        }
    }
}
```

Code for the function to take a picture

Here we discuss the code to define the function that will prompt the camera to take the picture.

The function has the code that will take the picture:

```
void takingpicture(){
```

Take a picture:

```
if (!cam.takePicture())
    Serial.println("Failed to snap!");
else
    Serial.println("Picture taken!");
```

Here we create the file to save:

```
char filename[13];
```

Here we save the file:

```
strcpy(filename, "IMAGE00.JPG");
for (int i = 0; i < 100; i++) {
    filename[5] = '0' + i/10;
    filename[6] = '0' + i%10;
```

Prepare the micro SD to save the files:

```
if (! SD.exists(filename)) {
    break;
    }
}
```

Open the file for preview:

```
File imgFile = SD.open(filename, FILE_WRITE);
```

Get the size of the file before saving:

```
uint16_t jpglen = cam.frameLength();
Serial.print("Storing ");
Serial.print(jpglen, DEC);
Serial.print(" byte image.");
```

Read the data from the file that was saved:

```
byte wCount = 0; // For counting # of writes
while (jpglen > 0) {
```

Write the file into the memory:

```
uint8_t *buffer;
uint8_t bytesToRead = min(32, jpglen);
buffer = cam.readPicture(bytesToRead);
imgFile.write(buffer, bytesToRead);
```

Display the file after saving:

```
if(++wCount >= 64) {
  Serial.print('.');
  wCount = 0;
}
```

Display the number of bytes read:

```
Serial.print(bytesToRead, DEC);
Serial.println(" bytes");
jpglen -= bytesToRead;
  }
```

Close the file which are open:

```
imgFile.close();
}
```

Controlling your camera from a web page

In this section, we will look ar how to control our camera from a web page in PHP and run a web server in the Raspberry Pi. We will need the following to run PHP files and web server:

- Running the Apache server on Raspberry Pi
- Installing PHP software

For the web page, for controlling we will have to create our PHP files in the following path: /var/www/html, for instance we need to edit the index.php file, and copy the following lines.

The following HTML file includes PHP:

```
<!DOCTYPE html>
<html>
 <head>
 <title>Control Camera</title>
 </head>
  <body>
```

Here we define the function to perform action for taking the picture:

```
<form  action="on.php">
  <button type="submit">Taking the picture</button>
  </form>
```

Here we define the action to taken if motion detected:

```
    <form action="off.php">
    <button type="submit">Motion</button>
    </form>
</body>
</html>
```

Calling the Python scripts from PHP

In this section, we need to call the Python script from the web page and execute the file that has the script:

```php
<?php
$prende= exec('sudo python on.py');
header('Location:index.php');
?>

<?php
$apaga = exec('sudo python motion.py');
header('Location:index.php');
?>
```

Code for Python scripts

On the server side, that is the Raspberry Pi, we have the Python scripts that will be called from the web page:

```python
import serial
import time
Arduino_1 = serial.Serial('/dev/ttyACM0',9600)
Arduino_1.open()
Command='H'
if command:
    Arduino_1.write(command)
Arduino_1.close()

import serial
import time
Arduino_1 = serial.Serial('/dev/ttyACM0',9600)
Arduino_1.open()
Command='L'
if command:
    Arduino_1.write(command)
Arduino_1.close()
```

If everything is configured perfectly, the following page will appear: in your favorite browser, type IP address of your `PI/index.php`:

Monitoring your USB camera for security in a network

In this section, we will create a project that allows us to monitor a USB camera that is connected to an Arduino YUN, which has a USB port and includes communication with Ethernet and Wi-Fi. So, it has many advantages. We will work on making a network between the Raspberry Pi and the Arduino YUN, so the main idea is to monitor the camera from a web page, from the Raspberry Pi. The page will be stored in the Raspberry Pi.

Configuring Arduino YUN

We will use a Logitech camera that supports the UVC protocol:

Now we will explain the steps to install our camera in the Arduino YUN:

- Connect the board to your Wi-Fi router
- Verify the IP address of the Arduino YUN

After we type the IP address, the following screen appears:

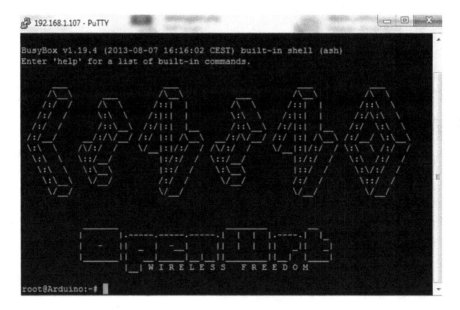

We will now issue a series of commands at the Command Prompt to complete the setup:

Update the package:

```
opkg update
```

Install the UVC protocol:

```
opkg install kmod-video-uvc
```

Install the camera driver:

```
opkg install fswebcam
```

Download the Mjpgstreamer:

```
wget http://www.custommobileapps.com.au/downloads/mjpgstreamer.Ipk
```

Install the Mjpgstreamer:

```
opkg install mjpg-streamer.ipk
```

To start the camera manually, use the following code:

```
mjpg_streamer -i "input_uvc.so -d /dev/video0 -r 640x480 -f 25" -o
"output_http.so -p 8080 -w /www/webcam" &
```

To start the camera automatically, we will use the following code:

Install the nano program:

```
opkg install nano
```

Enter the following file:

```
nano /etc/config/mjpg-streamer
```

Configure the camera with the following parameters:

```
config mjpg-streamer core
option enabled    "1"
option device     "/dev/video0"
option resolution "640x480"
option fps     "30"
option www     "/www/webcam"
option port    "8080"
```

Use the following command to start the service:

```
/etc/init.d/mjpg-streamer enable
/etc/init.d/mjpg-streamer stop
/etc/init.d/mjpg-streamer start
```

Monitoring from the MJPG-STREAMER server

Once you have accessed the server of the Arduino YUN, type the IP Address of your Arduino YUN, `http://Arduino.local:8080`, in your web browser. The results of the configuration are shown in the following screenshot:

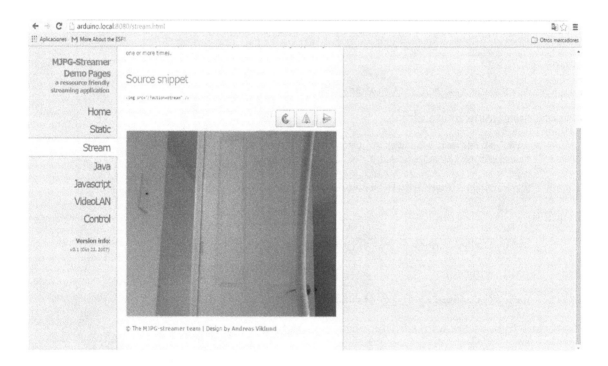

Monitoring the USB camera from the Raspberry Pi

With the camera connected to the Arduino YUN, now we can monitor in real time from a web page published in the Raspberry Pi.

Provide a title for the web page:

```
<html>
<head>
<title>Monitoring USB Camera</title>
```

We call the camera image by putting the IP address of the Arduino YUN:

```
</head>
<body>
<center>
<img src="http://192.168.1.107:8080/?action=stream"/>
</center>
</body>
</html>
```

Access the web page from a browser by typing the IP address of the Raspberry Pi (
`http://192.168.1.106/index.html`):

In the next section, we will look how to configure the connected devices and the hardware that will be interacting in a network.

The following image represents the network that we created with devices that can be monitored; for example, we monitor each room of a house, connect all the devices with a Wi-Fi network, and monitor them from the Raspberry Pi:

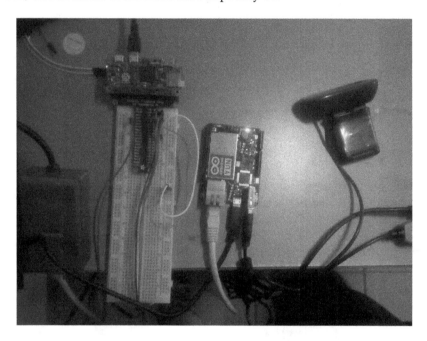

Summary

In this chapter, you have learned how to configure a web cam connected to the network and monitor your security system for the Internet of Things. We used your Arduino Board to connect the security camera, and Raspberry Pi Zero connected to the network to monitor the system. In the next chapter, we will integrate our system, the Raspberry Pi Zero, with Arduino, to build a complete system-connected device and monitor.

6

Building a Web Monitor and Controlling Devices from a Dashboard

In this chapter, we will talk about a very important part of this book, creating a web page that can control different kinds of devices from a dashboard. In an automated home there are different kinds of devices that could be controlled, for example: lamps, doors or windows, washing machines, and so on.

In this chapter, we will cover the following topics:

- Configuring MySQL database server
- Installing phpMyAdmin for administrating databases
- Datalogger with MySQL
- Dimming a LED
- Controlling the speed of a DC motor
- Controlling lights with electrical circuits
- Controlling door locks
- Controlling watering plants
- Remote access from anywhere to your Raspberry Pi Zero
- Controlling lights and measuring current consumption
- Controlling and monitoring Arduino, Wi-Fi and Ethernet shields, connected devices, and sensors from the Raspberry Pi Zero

Configuring MySQL database server

In this section, you will learn how to configure MySQL server in order to create a database and integrate everything in your dashboard, for recording data in a database.

Installing MySQL

Our Raspberry Pi Zero is being configured like a web server. In this section, we will install MySQL database server with the following command, so we can receive connections from clients, display data stored in a database, and use queries in SQL:

```
sudo apt-get install mysql-server
```

In the middle of the process it will ask you for the password of the root user:

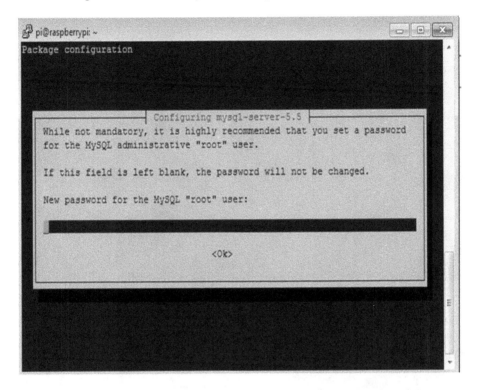

After the installation is complete, connect to MySQL and type the following command:

```
mysql -u root -p
```

Type the following command:

```
show databases;
```

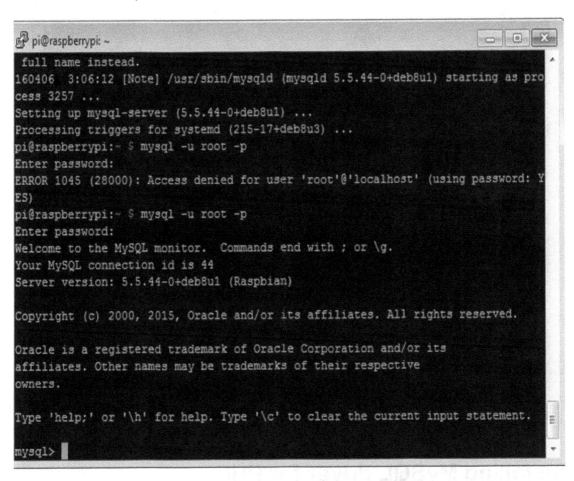

Here we can see databases of the system that are now installed in the server:

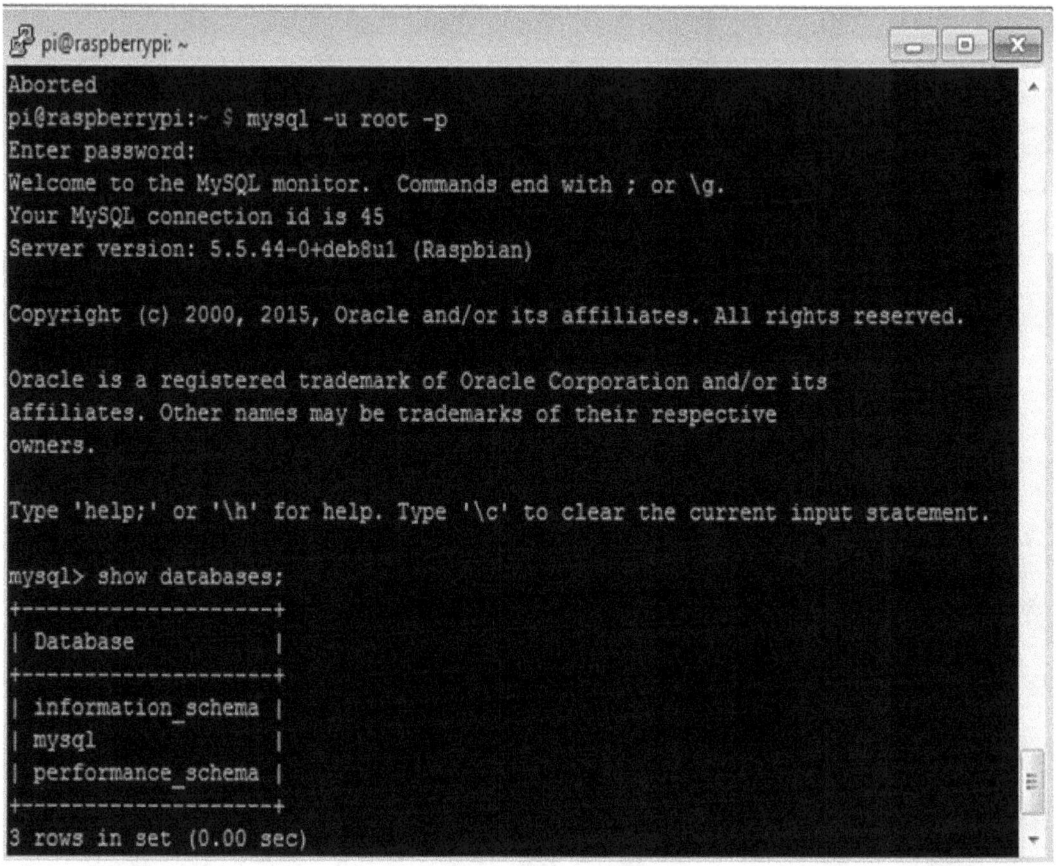

Installing MySQL driver for PHP

It's important to install our driver to communicate PHP5 with MySQL database server, to do that we will need MySQL driver for PHP to access MySQL database, execute this command to install PHP-MySQL Driver.

```
sudo apt-get install php5 php5-mysql
```

Testing PHP and MySQL

In this section, we will make a simple page to test PHP and MySQL with the following command:

```
sudo nano /var/www/html/hellodb.php
```

```
pi@raspberrypi: ~                                                   [_][□][X]
pi@raspberrypi:~ $ <body>
-bash: syntax error near unexpected token `newline'
pi@raspberrypi:~ $ <p> list of databases:</p>
-bash: syntax error near unexpected token `newline'
pi@raspberrypi:~ $ <?php
-bash: ?php: No such file or directory
pi@raspberrypi:~ $ $link = mysql_connect('localhost', 'root', 'ruben');
-bash: syntax error near unexpected token `('
pi@raspberrypi:~ $ $res = mysql_query("SHOW DATABASES");
-bash: syntax error near unexpected token `('
pi@raspberrypi:~ $
pi@raspberrypi:~ $ while ($row = mysql_fetch_assoc($res)) {
-bash: syntax error near unexpected token `('
pi@raspberrypi:~ $         echo $row['Database'] . "<br>";
[Database] . <br>
pi@raspberrypi:~ $ }
-bash: syntax error near unexpected token `}'
pi@raspberrypi:~ $ ?>
-bash: syntax error near unexpected token `newline'
pi@raspberrypi:~ $ </body>
-bash: syntax error near unexpected token `newline'
pi@raspberrypi:~ $ </html>
-bash: syntax error near unexpected token `newline'
pi@raspberrypi:~ $ sudo nano /var/www/html/hellodb.php
```

The following screenshot has the script that has the code to access the database, connect to the server, and get the data from it:

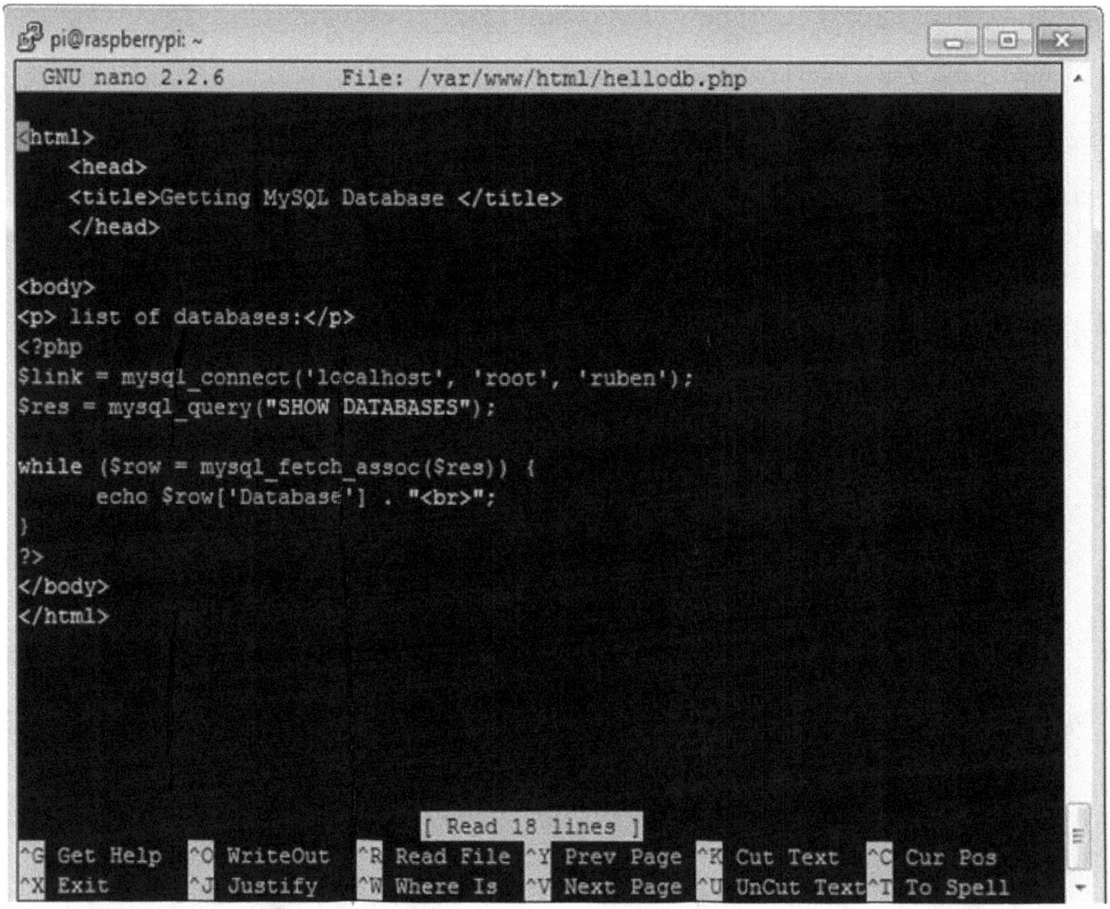

```
 GNU nano 2.2.6              File: /var/www/html/hellodb.php

<html>
    <head>
    <title>Getting MySQL Database </title>
    </head>

<body>
<p> list of databases:</p>
<?php
$link = mysql_connect('localhost', 'root', 'ruben');
$res = mysql_query("SHOW DATABASES");

while ($row = mysql_fetch_assoc($res)) {
      echo $row['Database'] . "<br>";
}
?>
</body>
</html>




                         [ Read 18 lines ]
^G Get Help   ^O WriteOut   ^R Read File  ^Y Prev Page  ^K Cut Text   ^C Cur Pos
^X Exit       ^J Justify    ^W Where Is   ^V Next Page  ^U UnCut Text ^T To Spell
```

To test the page and connection between PHP and MySQL, type the IP address of your Raspberry Pi: `http://192.168.1.105/hellodb.php`. The page that should similar to the following screenshot:

Installing PhpMyAdmin for administrating databases

In this section, we will talk about how to configure your PhpMyAdmin to administrate your database from a remote panel. It's important that we install the client and the module PHP5 in the Apache server, so type the following command:

```
sudo apt-get install mysql-client php5-mysql
```

Next we will install the `phpmyadmin` package with the following command:

```
sudo apt install phpmyadmin
```

In the following screenshot, we can see the configuration of the server; in this case, we need to select **apache2**:

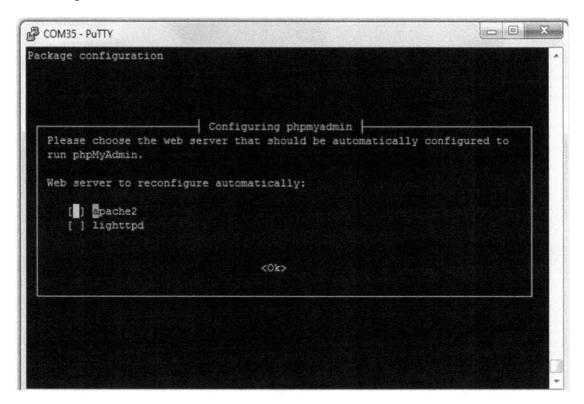

We choose the apache2 server:

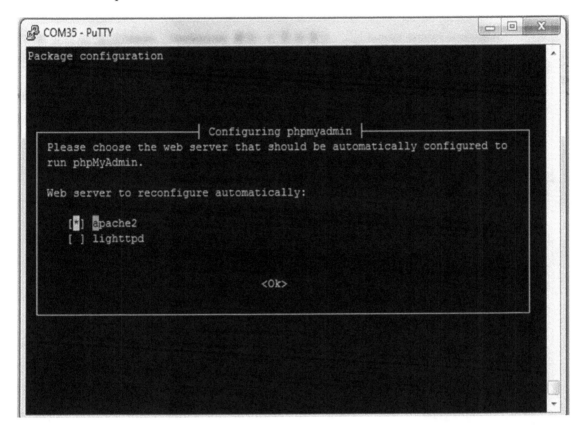

After that we can select the database:

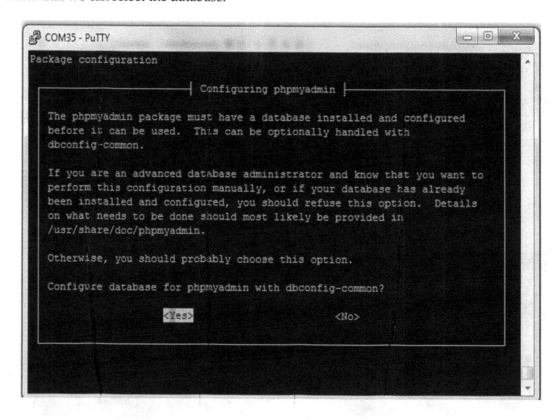

We choose the option **<No>**:

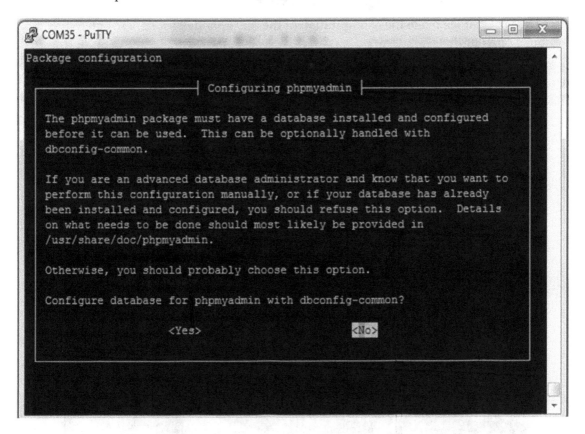

Configuring the Apache server

It's necessary that we make the configuration of the file `apache2.conf`. First go to the Terminal on your Pi:

```
sudo nano /etc/apache2/apache2.conf
```

In the following screen, we need to add the code:

```
Include /etc/phpmyadmin/apche.conf
```

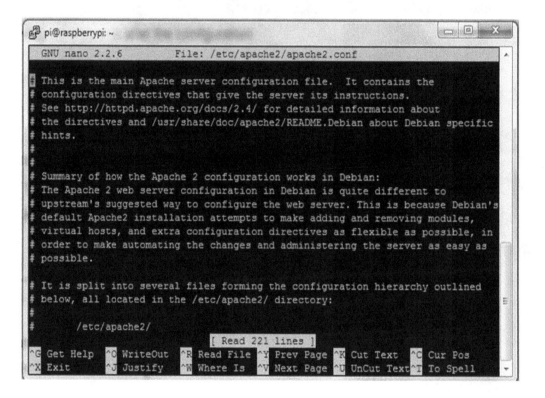

We include the following line in the bottom of the file:

```
Include /etc/phpmyadmin/apche.conf
```

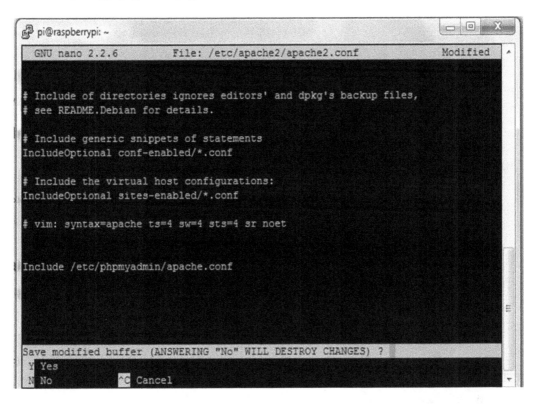

We have finally finished installing our Apache server, and we are now ready for the next step.

Entering to the phpMyAdmin remote panel

After we have configured the server we will enter the phpMyAdmin remote panel, we need to open our favorite web browser and type the IP Address of our Raspberry Pi: `http://(Raspberry Pi Address)/phpmyadmin`, which will show the following screen:

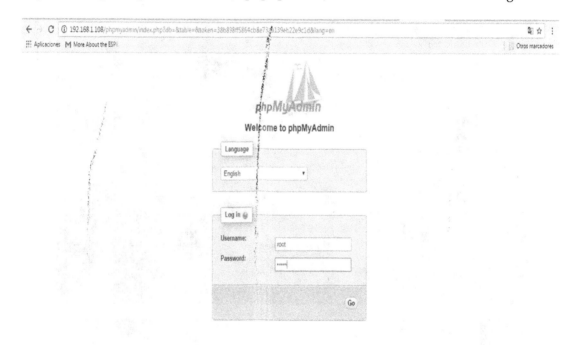

Showing the Arduinobd database

The following screenshot shows the database created in the server:

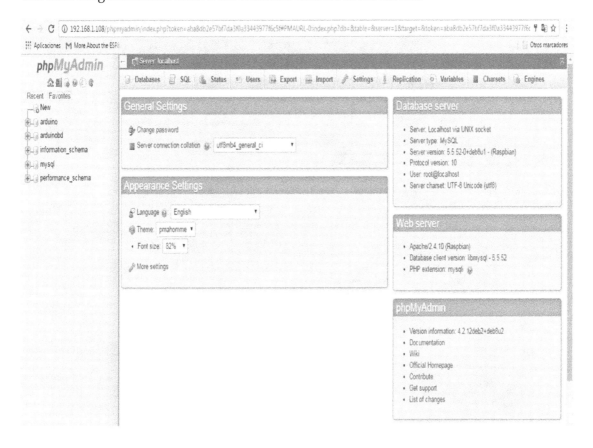

The following screenshot shows the table **measurements**, columns, **id**, **temperature** and **humidity**:

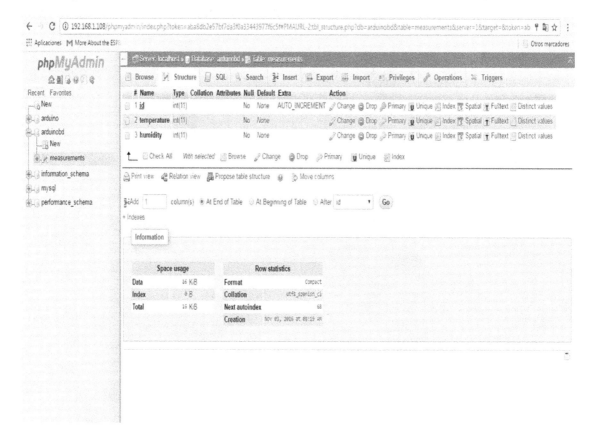

Sending data from Arduino and the Ethernet shield to the web server

We use an Arduino and the Ethernet Shield connected to the network, Arduino sends data to the web server published in the Raspberry Pi Zero.

You can now either copy the code inside a file called `arduino_xaamp_mysql.ino`, or just get the complete code from the code folder of this book:

We enter the Ip address of the Arduino UNO:

```
IPAddress ip(192,168,1,50);
```

We configure the IPAddress of our Raspberry Pi Zero:

```
IPAddress server(192,168,1,108);
```

We need to connect to the web server:

```
if (client.connect(server, 80))
```

These lines define the HTTP request from the remote server:

```
client.println("GET /datalogger1.php?temp=" + temp + "&hum=" + hum + "
HTTP/1.1");
    client.println("Host: 192.168.1.108");
    client.println("Connection: close");
    client.println();
```

The rest of the code is shown in the following lines:

```
// Include libraries
#include <SPI.h>
#include <Ethernet.h>
#include "DHT.h"
// Enter a MAC address for your controller below.
byte mac[] = { 0x90, 0xA2, 0xDA, 0x0E, 0xFE, 0x40 };
// DHT11 sensor pins
#define DHTPIN 7
#define DHTTYPE DHT11
IPAddress ip(192,168,1,50);
IPAddress server(192,168,1,108);
EthernetClient client;
DHT dht(DHTPIN, DHTTYPE);
void setup() {
  // Open serial communications
  Serial.begin(9600);
      Ethernet.begin(mac, ip);
  Serial.print("IP address: ");
  Serial.println(Ethernet.localIP());
  delay(1000);
  Serial.println("Conectando...");
}
void loop()
```

```
{
   float h = dht.readHumidity();
   float t = dht.readTemperature();
   String temp = String((int) t);
   String hum = String((int) h);
     if (client.connect(server, 80)) {
     if (client.connected()) {
        Serial.println("conectado");
```

Make an HTTP request:

```
      client.println("GET /datalogger1.php?temp=" + temp + "&hum=" + hum +
" HTTP/1.1");
      client.println("Host: 192.168.1.108");
      client.println("Connection: close");
      client.println();
   }
   else {
      // If you didn't get a connection to the server
      Serial.println("fallo la conexion");
   }
```

Thes lines define how the instance of the client can read the response:

```
while (client.connected()) {
   while (client.available()) {
   char c = client.read();
   Serial.print(c);
   }
}
```

If the server's disconnected, stop the client:

```
if (!client.connected()) {
   Serial.println();
   Serial.println("desconectado.");
   client.stop();
   }
}
```

Repeat every second:

```
delay(5000);
}
```

Here we can see the hardware that we used:

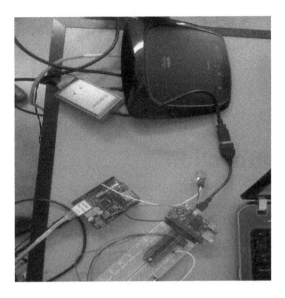

Datalogger with MySQL

In the following section, we will build a Datalogger that will record the data temperature and humidity in the server so that we can get data whenever we want and display it in a web page.

Programming the script software

In the following code, we have a script that will communicate with the Arduino board, and it is installed in the server.

You can now either copy the code inside a file called datalogger1.php, or just get the complete code from the folder for this project:

```php
<?php
if (isset($_GET["temp"]) && isset($_GET["hum"])) {
$temperature = intval($_GET["temp"]);
$humidity = intval($_GET["hum"]);
$con=mysql_connect("localhost","root","ruben","arduinobd");
mysql_select_db('arduinobd',$con);
    if(mysql_query("INSERT INTO measurements (temperature, humidity)
```

```
VALUES ('$temperature', '$humidity');")){
    echo "Data were saved";
    }
    else {
    echo "Fail the recorded data";
    }
mysql_close($con);
}
?>
```

Testing the connection

After we have installed the file of the script, we need to open a web browser in your computer and type the IP address of your `Raspberry Pi/datalogger1.php?temp=70&hum=100`, the link will look like as **(http://192.168.1.108/datalogger1.php?temp=70&hum=100)**:

Datos guardados

The following screenshot shows the results of the data saved on the database:

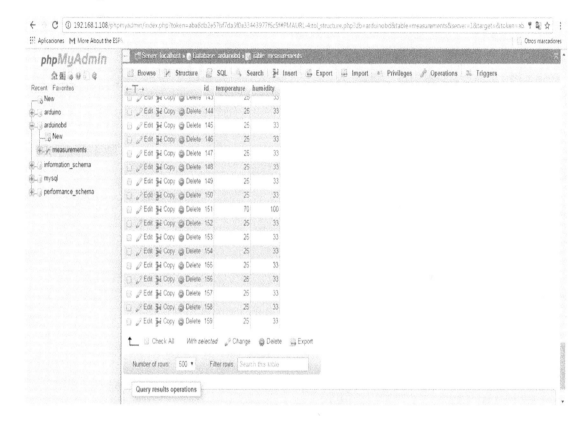

The following screenshot shows the table of the data:

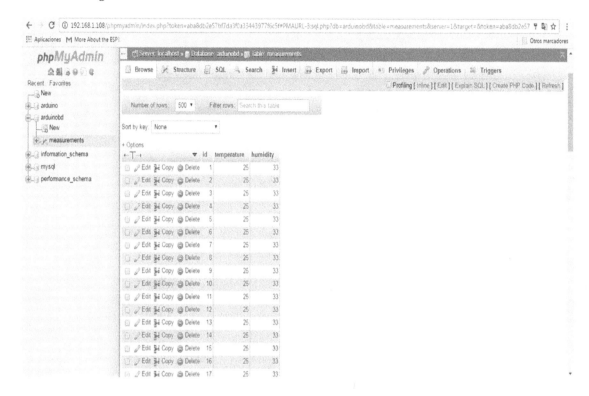

Data queries from the database

It's important to have data recorded and to make some queries to have the data show in the web page.

Software for the scripts

Here we have the scripts that we used to show the data in the page:

You can now either copy the code inside a file called `query1.php`, or just get the complete code from the folder for this project:

```html
<!DOCTYPE html>
  <html>
    <body>
<h1>Clik on the buttons to get Data from  MySQL</h1>
<form action="query1.php" method="get">
<input type="submit" value="Get all Data">
</form>
</br>

<form action="query2.php" method="get">
<input type="submit"value="Humidity <= 15">
</form>
</br>

<form action="query3.php" method="get">
<input type="submit" value="Temperature <=25">
</form>
</br>
<?php

$con=mysql_connect("localhost","root","ruben","arduinobd");
mysql_select_db('arduinobd',$con);
$result = mysql_query("SELECT * FROM measurements");
echo "<table border='1'>
<tr>
<th>Measurements</th>
<th>Temperature (°C)</th>
<th>Humidity (%)</th>
</tr>";
while($row = mysql_fetch_array($result)) {
  echo "<tr>";
  echo "<td>" . $row['id'] . "</td>";
  echo "<td>" . $row['temperature'] . "</td>";
  echo "<td>" . $row['humidity'] . "</td>";
  echo "</tr>";
}
echo "</table>";
mysql_close($con);
?>
</body>
</html>
```

In the following screenshot we have the data:

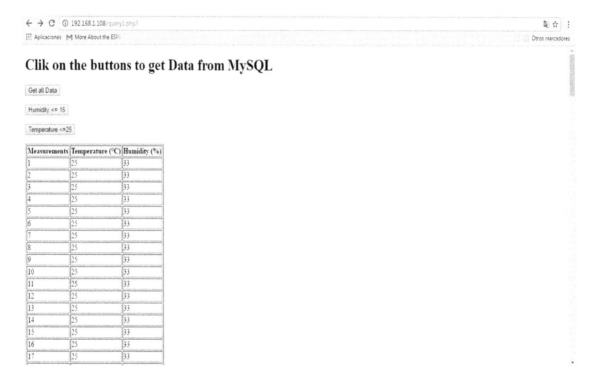

Scripts for specific data to be displayed

In the following lines we see that we can make some SQL queries to have information of specific values and get the values from the temperature and humidity:

```php
<?php
$con=mysql_connect("localhost","root","ruben","arduinobd");
mysql_select_db('arduinobd',$con);
$result = mysql_query("SELECT * FROM measurements where humidity <= 15
order by id");
echo "<table border='1'>
<tr>
<th>Measurements</th>
<th>Temperature (°C)</th>
<th>Humidity (%)</th>
</tr>";
while($row = mysql_fetch_array($result)) {
  echo "<tr>";
```

```php
    echo "<td>" . $row['id'] . "</td>";
    echo "<td>" . $row['temperature'] . "</td>";
    echo "<td>" . $row['humidity'] . "</td>";
    echo "</tr>";
}
echo "</table>";
mysql_close($con);
?>
```

Query for recording temperature

In this section, we will create a query to get temperature measurements. We call the server reference to the `localhost`, in this case it is the Raspberry Pi zero device, the user, and the name of the database:

```php
<?php
$con=mysql_connect("localhost","root","ruben","arduinobd");
mysql_select_db('arduinobd',$con);
$result = mysql_query("SELECT * FROM measurements where temperature <= 25
order by id");
echo "<table border='1'>
<tr>
<th>Measurements</th>
<th>Temperature (°C)</th>
<th>Humidity (%)</th>
</tr>";
while($row = mysql_fetch_array($result)) {
    echo "<tr>";
    echo "<td>" . $row['id'] . "</td>";
    echo "<td>" . $row['temperature'] . "</td>";
    echo "<td>" . $row['humidity'] . "</td>";
    echo "</tr>";
}
echo "</table>";
mysql_close($con);
?>
```

The result of the queries is shown in the following screenshot:

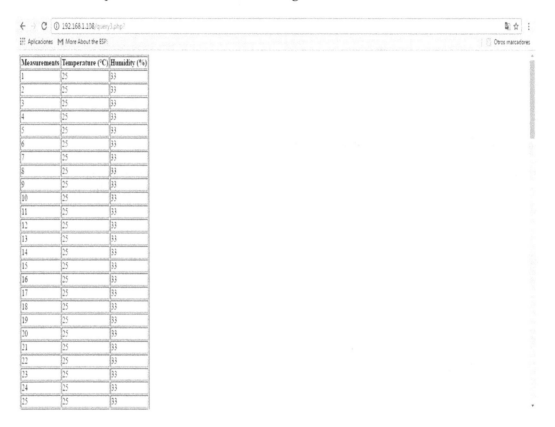

Controlling and dimming a LED

In this section, we will discuss a project that can be applied to a home automation. We will dim an LED of DC, this can done to a lamp in a house. The LED will change its brightness, and we connect the LED to the **GPIO18** of the Raspberry Pi in series with a resistor of *330* ohms.

Software requirements

First we need to install the `pigpio` package. In the Terminal, type the following:

```
wget abyz.co.uk/rpi/pigpio/pigpio.zip
```

Then unzip the package:

```
unzip pigpio.zip
```

After that, navigate to the unzipped folder with the following:

```
cd PIGPIO
```

Type the following to execute the command:

```
Make
```

Finally install the file:

```
sudo make install
```

Testing the LED

In this section, we will test the sensor with a script in **Node.js**:

```
var Gpio = require('pigpio').Gpio;

// Create led instance
var led = new Gpio(18, {mode: Gpio.OUTPUT});
var dutyCycle = 0;
// Go from 0 to maximum brightness
setInterval(function () {
  led.pwmWrite(dutyCycle);
  dutyCycle += 5;
  if (dutyCycle > 255) {
    dutyCycle = 0;
  }
}, 20);
```

We can already test this code, navigate into the folder of this project with a Terminal on the Pi, and type the following:

```
sudo npm install pigpio
```

This will install the required `node.js` module to control the LED. Then, type the following:

```
sudo node led_test.js
```

This is the final result:

Controlling the LED from an interface

In this section, we will control the LED from a web page. For which we will use HTML to make the interface with the user, using `node.js`.

Let's take a look at the Node.js files that are included in the following code:

```
// Modules
var Gpio = require('pigpio').Gpio;
var express = require('express');
// Express app
var app = express();

// Use public directory
app.use(express.static('public'));
// Create led instance
var led = new Gpio(18, {mode: Gpio.OUTPUT});

// Routes
app.get('/', function (req, res) {

  res.sendfile(__dirname + '/public/interface.html');
```

```
});
app.get('/set', function (req, res) {

  // Set LED
  dutyCycle = req.query.dutyCycle;
  led.pwmWrite(dutyCycle);

  // Answer
  answer = {
    dutyCycle: dutyCycle
  };
  res.json(answer);

});

// Start server
app.listen(3000, function () {
  console.log('Raspberry Pi Zero LED control');
});
```

It's now finally time to test our application! First, grab all the code from this book's repository and navigate to the folder of the project like before. Then, install `express` with the following command:

sudo npm install express

When this is done, start the server with the following command:

sudo node led_control.js

You can now test the project, open the web browser in your computer, and type the link – `http://(Raspberry PI)/set?dutyCycle=20`, and we can see that the LED changes with the value.

Then open your web browser with `http://192.168.1.108:3000` and you should see the control in a basic web page:

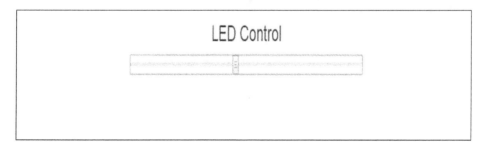

Controlling the speed of a DC motor

It's common to have a window or a garage door in a house. We need to automate these kinds of devices, so that we can move these objects with a DC motor. In this section, we will see how to connect a DC motor to the Raspberry Pi. To do this, we will use a L293D circuit to control the motor.

First we will see how to connect the motor to our Raspberry Pi Zero board. In the following diagram, we can see the pins out of the LD293 chip:

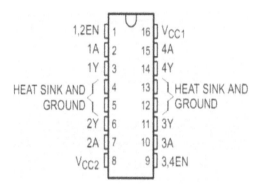

We basically need to connect the components of the circuit, as follows:

- **GPIO14** of the Raspberry Pi to pin **1A**
- **GPIO15** of the Raspberry Pi to pin **2A**
- **GPIO18** of the Raspberry Pi to pin **1, 2EN**
- **DC motor** to pin **1Y** and **2Y**
- **5V** of the Raspberry Pi to **VCC1**
- **GND** of the Raspberry Pi to **GND**
- Adapter regulator to **VCC2** and **GND**

The following image shows the results:

We will now test the speed of the DC motor from 0 to the highest speed:

```
// Modules
var Gpio = require('pigpio').Gpio;
// Create motor instance
var motorSpeed = new Gpio(18, {mode: Gpio.OUTPUT});
var motorDirectionOne = new Gpio(14, {mode: Gpio.OUTPUT});
var motorDirectionTwo = new Gpio(15, {mode: Gpio.OUTPUT})

// Init motor direction
motorDirectionOne.digitalWrite(0);
motorDirectionTwo.digitalWrite(1);
var dutyCycle = 0;

// Go from 0 to maximum brightness
setInterval(function () {
  motorSpeed.pwmWrite(dutyCycle);
  dutyCycle += 5;
  if (dutyCycle > 255) {
    dutyCycle = 0;
  }
}, 20);
```

Here we have the code for this application to control the DC motor using the interface in a web page:

```javascript
// Modules
var Gpio = require('pigpio').Gpio;
var express = require('express');

// Express app
var app = express();
// Use public directory
app.use(express.static('public'));

// Create led instance
var motorSpeed = new Gpio(18, {mode: Gpio.OUTPUT});
var motorDirectionOne = new Gpio(14, {mode: Gpio.OUTPUT});
var motorDirectionTwo = new Gpio(15, {mode: Gpio.OUTPUT});

// Routes
app.get('/', function (req, res) {

  res.sendfile(__dirname + '/public/interface.html');

});

app.get('/set', function (req, res) {
  // Set motor speed
  speed = req.query.speed;
  motorSpeed.pwmWrite(speed);

  // Set motor direction
  motorDirectionOne.digitalWrite(0);
  motorDirectionTwo.digitalWrite(1);

// Answer
  answer = {
    speed: speed
  };
  res.json(answer);

});

// Start server
app.listen(3000, function () {
  console.log('Raspberry Pi Zero Motor control started!');
});
```

We see the interface of the user in the following code:

```
$( document ).ready(function() {

  $( "#motor-speed" ).mouseup(function() {

    // Get value
    var speed = $('#motor-speed').val();

    // Set new value
    $.get('/set?speed=' + speed);

  });


});

<!DOCTYPE html>
<html>

<head>
  <script src="https://code.jquery.com/jquery-2.2.4.min.js"></script>
  <link rel="stylesheet"
href="https://maxcdn.bootstrapcdn.com/bootstrap/3.3.6/css/bootstrap.min.css
">
  <script
src="https://maxcdn.bootstrapcdn.com/bootstrap/3.3.6/js/bootstrap.min.js"><
/script>
  <script src="js/interface.js"></script>
  <link rel="stylesheet" href="css/style.css">
  <meta name="viewport" content="width=device-width, initial-scale=1">
</head>
<body>

<div id="container">

  <h3>Motor Control</h3>

  <div class='row'>

    <div class='col-md-4'></div>
    <div class='col-md-4 text-center'>
     <input id="motor-speed" type="range" value="0" min="0" max="255"
step="1">
    </div>
    <div class='col-md-4'></div>

  </div>
```

```
      </div>

      </body>
      </html>
```

To test the application, you need to open the web browser in your computer with the link, `http://192.168.1.108:3000`, and then you need to replace the IP Address of your Pi. Here we have the interface for this:

Controlling Lights with electrical circuits

In the following sections, you will find ideas on how to dive into more projects that control other devices in the house.

Electrical appliances

In houses we have electrical appliances, for example, lamps, washing machines, heaters, and other appliances that we only need to turn on or off. In this section, we will learn how to control a lamp connected to the Raspberry Pi Zero, using electrical circuits for interfacing the signal. We will use an **optocoupler** such as MOC3011, and a **Triac**. The following figure shows the circuit of the application:

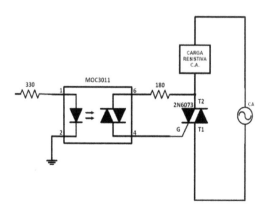

Here we have the final project connected to the Raspberry pi Zero:

Here we have the JavaScript code for controlling the device:

```
// Modules
var express = require('express');

// Express app
var app = express();

// Pin
var lampPin = 12;

// Use public directory
app.use(express.static('public'));

// Routes
app.get('/', function (req, res) {

  res.sendfile(__dirname + '/public/interface.html');

});

app.get('/on', function (req, res) {
```

```
    piREST.digitalWrite(lampPin, 1);

    // Answer
    answer = {
      status: 1
    };
    res.json(answer);

});

app.get('/off', function (req, res) {

    piREST.digitalWrite(lampPin, 0);

    // Answer
    answer = {
      status: 0
    };
    res.json(answer);

});

// aREST
var piREST = require('pi-arest')(app);
piREST.set_id('34f5eQ');
piREST.set_name('my_rpi_zero');

// Start server
app.listen(3000, function () {
  console.log('Raspberry Pi Zero lamp control started!');
});
```

We need an interface that can control the lamp from the web page in the HTML language:

```
<!DOCTYPE html>
<html>

<head>
  <script src="https://code.jquery.com/jquery-2.2.4.min.js"></script>
  <link rel="stylesheet"
href="https://maxcdn.bootstrapcdn.com/bootstrap/3.3.6/css/bootstrap.min.css
">
  <script
src="https://maxcdn.bootstrapcdn.com/bootstrap/3.3.6/js/bootstrap.min.js"><
/script>
  <script src="js/script.js"></script>
  <link rel="stylesheet" href="css/style.css">
  <meta name="viewport" content="width=device-width, initial-scale=1">
```

```
</head>

<body>

<div id="container">

  <h3>Lamp Control</h3>

  <div class='row'>

    <div class='col-md-4'></div>
    <div class='col-md-2'>
      <button id='on' class='btn btn-block btn-primary'>On</button>
    </div>
    <div class='col-md-2'>
      <button id='off' class='btn btn-block btn-warning'>Off</button>
    </div>
    <div class='col-md-4'></div>

  </div>

</div>

</body>
</html>
```

After entering the web browser, we will see the following interface:

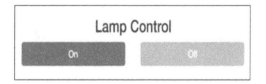

Other appliances

In this section, we will show other applications that you can consider creating and controlling, and then use them in the home or different areas.

Control a door lock

In this section, we will see other appliances that can be controlled from an interface and connected to the Raspberry pi. In the house we can control a door lock from a web interface:

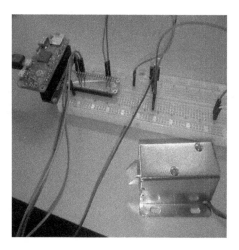

Control watering plants

Another appliance that we can control is watering plants with a Plastic Water Solenoid Valve – 12V, connected to the Raspberry Pi:

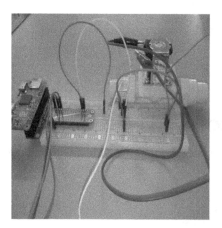

With this project we can make an automated watering system, add a humidity sensor, and program the time that the plants of the garden will be watered.

Remote access from anywhere to your Raspberry Pi Zero

If we want access to our Raspberry Pi from outside our network, we need to do the following:

- Check if our modem has a public IP address
- Investigate the address that we'll be using in our browser
- Type `http://whatismyipaddress.com/` in our browser

IP provided by the ISP are genteraly dynamic IP which changes after some time. In our cases we need to have static addresses which does not change occasionally.

How to access our modem to configure it

Access our modem via the Ip address (gateway) and go to the port addressing part. Configure port *80* that points to our web server (put the IP address of our account), this IP address is the one that automatically assigns the DHCP server of our system.

Here we have some ports that can be forwarded from the modem-router:

Application	External Port	Internal Port	Protocol
HTTP	80	80	TCP
FTP	21	21	TCP
FTP-Data	20	20	TCP
Telnet	23	23	TCP
SMTP	25	25	TCP
TFTP	69	69	UDP
finger	79	79	TCP
NTP	123	123	UDP
POP3	110	110	TCP
NNTP	119	119	TCP
SNMP	161	161	UDP
CVS	2401	2401	TCP
SMS	2701	2701	TCP
SMS-rmctl	2702	2702	TCP

To get the gateway IP address, type the `ipconfig` command, you need to have admin rights. After this, type `http://gatewayip_addres` in the web browser of your `router.1`:

This is an example of what you'd see if you had a Linksys router, yours may be a different interface:

To open a port we need to configure our router to give permissions for entering from outside, so we need to give permission in our router:

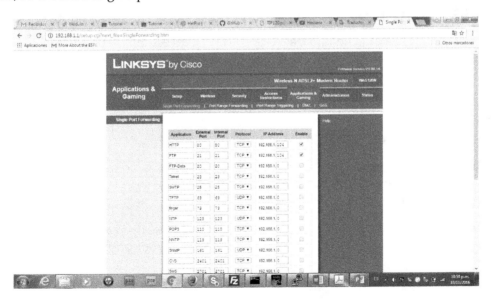

This screenshot shows the final results, how to open a port number 3000, and the name of the application node:

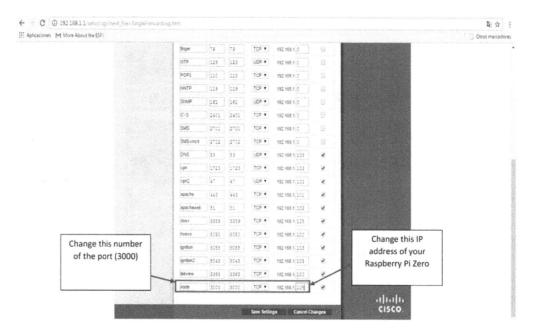

Configuring Dynamic DNS

We need to configure a domain name service so we can access our web server by typing the name of our domain (it is very difficult to learn the IP addresses of the web pages). That's why **Domain Name Servers (DNS)** were created. Follow the next section to create a domain.

You may want to access your IoT control panels away from home. In that case, your web server will need to become a host on the Internet.

This is not a straightforward thing since it's behind the router in your home. Your ISP generally does not give you a static public IP address because most users are simply accessing the web, not serving web pages.

Therefore, the public side of your router is given an IP address that can change from time to time. If you browse to <whatsmyip...>, you will see what your public IP is currently.

Tomorrow it could be different. For setting up external access, you can do one of two things. If you want to simulate having a static IP, you can use a service such as Dynamic DNS. If you just want to "try out" external access, you can open a port on your router

Benefits of having Dynamic DNS:

- One solution is to install a client that will allow the public IP to make it fixed. The client function (software that is installed on a computer), maintains communication with the site www.no-ip.org.
- When the IP address of our modem changes, the client takes that IP change.
- This allows our domain name to always point to our public IP address. The software that is installed is called: No-IP DUC.

Creating an account at No-ip.org

In the following screenshot we can see the Enhance dynamic DNS setting up:

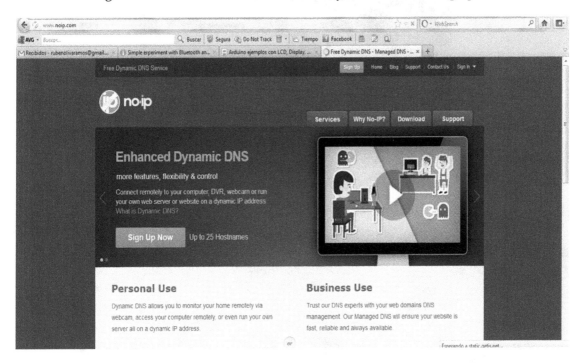

Controlling lights and measuring current consumption

Now in this section we will explain how to control and monitor your current consumption when the light is on or off. Using your Arduino Wi-Fi shield from a web page, we will monitor this variable. When the light is off it looks as follows:

When the light is on it looks as follows:

You can now either copy the code inside a file called
Controlling_lights_Current_Consumption.ino, or just get the complete code from
the folder of this book.

Define variables and functions to monitor and control:

```
#define NUMBER_VARIABLES 2
#define NUMBER_FUNCTIONS 1
```

Import libraries to use:

```
#include <Adafruit_CC3000.h>
#include <SPI.h>
#include <CC3000_MDNS.h>
#include <aREST.h>
```

Configure the relay to activate:

```
const int relay_pin = 8;
```

Variables to calculate the current:

```
float amplitude_current;
float effective_value;
float effective_voltage = 110;
float effective_power;
float zero_sensor;
```

We define the pins for configuring the module:

```
#define ADAFRUIT_CC3000_IRQ    3
#define ADAFRUIT_CC3000_VBAT   5
#define ADAFRUIT_CC3000_CS     10
Adafruit_CC3000 cc3000 = Adafruit_CC3000(ADAFRUIT_CC3000_CS,
ADAFRUIT_CC3000_IRQ, ADAFRUIT_CC3000_VBAT);
```

We create the instance:

```
aREST rest = aREST();
```

We define the SSID and the password of your network:

```
#define WLAN_SSID       "xxxxxxxx"
#define WLAN_PASS       "xxxxxxxx"
#define WLAN_SECURITY   WLAN_SEC_WPA2
```

We configure the port of the server:

```
#define LISTEN_PORT 80
```

Instance of the server:

```
Adafruit_CC3000_Server restServer(LISTEN_PORT);
MDNSResponder mdns;
```

Variables that are used:

```
int power;
int light;
```

Publish the variables that are used:

```
void setup(void)
{
  Serial.begin(115200);
  rest.variable("light",&light);
  rest.variable("power",&power);
```

Set the relay pin that is the output:

```
  pinMode(relay_pin,OUTPUT);
```

Calibrate the current sensor:

```
  zero_sensor = getSensorValue(A1);
```

We declare the id and the name of the device:

```
  rest.set_id("001");
  rest.set_name("control");
```

In this part, we check if the device is connected:

```
  if (!cc3000.begin())
  {
    while(1);
  }

  if (!cc3000.connectToAP(WLAN_SSID, WLAN_PASS, WLAN_SECURITY)) {
    while(1);
  }
  while (!cc3000.checkDHCP())
  {
    delay(100);
  }
```

In this part, we define the request for communication:

```
  if (!mdns.begin("arduino", cc3000)) {
    while(1);
  }
  displayConnectionDetails();
```

Lets's start the server:

```
  restServer.begin();
  Serial.println(F("Listening for connections..."));
}
```

We read the sensors:

```
void loop() {
   float sensor_reading = analogRead(A0);
   light = (int)(sensor_reading/1024*100);
   float sensor_value = getSensorValue(A1);
```

We make the calculus of the current and acquire the signals:

```
amplitude_current = (float)(sensor_value-zero_sensor)/1024*5/185*1000000;
effective_value = amplitude_current/1.414;
effective_power = abs(effective_value*effective_voltage/1000);
power = (int)effective_power;
mdns.update();
```

We define incoming requests:

```
Adafruit_CC3000_ClientRef client = restServer.available();
   rest.handle(client);
}
```

We display the IP Address configuration:

```
bool displayConnectionDetails(void)
{
   uint32_t ipAddress, netmask, gateway, dhcpserv, dnsserv;
   if(!cc3000.getIPAddress(&ipAddress, &netmask, &gateway, &dhcpserv,
&dnsserv))
   {
     Serial.println(F("Unable to retrieve the IP Address!\r\n"));
     return false;
   }
   else
   {
     Serial.print(F("\nIP Addr: "));  cc3000.printIPdotsRev(ipAddress);
     Serial.print(F("\nNetmask: "));  cc3000.printIPdotsRev(netmask);
     Serial.print(F("\nGateway: "));  cc3000.printIPdotsRev(gateway);
     Serial.print(F("\nDHCPsrv: "));  cc3000.printIPdotsRev(dhcpserv);
     Serial.print(F("\nDNSserv: "));  cc3000.printIPdotsRev(dnsserv);
     Serial.println();
     return true;
   }
}
```

Function of the current sensor that calculates the average of certain measurements and returns the current calculus:

```
float getSensorValue(int pin)
{
```

```
int sensorValue;
float avgSensor = 0;
int nb_measurements = 100;
for (int i = 0; i < nb_measurements; i++) {
  sensorValue = analogRead(pin);
  avgSensor = avgSensor + float(sensorValue);
}
avgSensor = avgSensor/float(nb_measurements);
return avgSensor;
}
```

Building the interface to control and monitor

Here we have the code for displaying the interface that controls the lights and monitoring the current with the sensor:

Installing Jade for Node.js

It's important to configure the Jade interface applied in this project. To do that we just type the following command:

```
npm install arest express jade
```

If it's necessary, we type the following command in case your system requires that update:

```
npm install pug
```

Interface for controlling and monitoring

First, we define the header of the page and add the HTML tag:

```
doctype
html
  head
    title Control and monitoring
```

We define the links for the functions for jQuery and Bootstrap:

```
link(rel='stylesheet', href='/css/interface.css')
    link(rel='stylesheet',
href="https://maxcdn.bootstrapcdn.com/bootstrap/3.3.0/css/bootstrap.min.css
")
    script(src="https://code.jquery.com/jquery-2.1.1.min.js")
    script(src="/js/interface.js")
```

We display the buttons to control in the web page:

```
body
  .container
    h1 Controlling lights
    .row.voffset
      .col-md-6
        button.btn.btn-block.btn-lg.btn-primary#1 On
      .col-md-6
        button.btn.btn-block.btn-lg.btn-danger#2 Off
    .row
```

Display the power and light level:

```
    .col-md-4
      h3#powerDisplay Power:
    .col-md-4
      h3#lightDisplay Light level:
    .col-md-4
      h3#status Offline
```

Now we will run the application, as we can see in the following screenshot. The server is open on port 3000, when it starts to send the request to the board, type the address on your web browser: `http://localhost:3000`. It shows the web page with both buttons and the device is connected and is online:

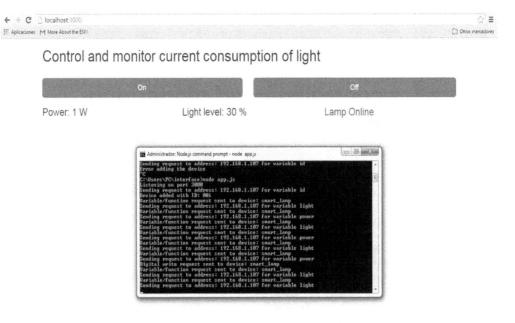

Click on the blue **On** button to activate the light on the board, after some seconds we can see that the power increases:

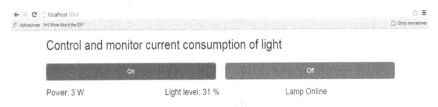

Click on the red **Off** button, after some seconds the power goes down until *0 W*, this means that everything is working perfectly well:

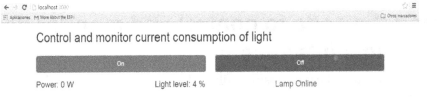

Controlling and monitoring Arduino, Wi-Fi, and Ethernet shields on connected devices and sensors

In previous sections, we saw how to control and monitor our Arduino boards from a web page using `node.js` running on a computer in Windows. In this section, we will use our fantastic Raspberry Pi Zero with Node.js installed on it and run the JavaScript application inside the board.

I have seen the potential of the board instead of using a personal computer installed as a web server, with this experience making this projects I want tell that the application is more efficient using our Raspberry Pi Zero running on it.

We will see how to control more than one device in a single dashboard using different devices, such as the following:

- Wi-Fi shield
- ESP8266 module
- Ethernet shield

Building the code to control and monitor devices from a single interface

You can now either copy the code inside a file called `app.js`, or just get the complete code from the folder for this project.

Configure the outputs of the devices connected in the system:

```
$.getq('queue', '/lamp_control/mode/8/o');
$.getq('queue', '/lamp_control2/mode/5/o');
```

Start the function to control:

```
$(document).ready(function() {
```

We make the GET request with the aREST API for ON:

```
// Function to control lamp Ethernet Shield
  $("#1").click(function() {
    $.getq('queue', '/lamp_control/digital/8/1');
  });
```

We make the GET request with the AREST API for OFF:

```
  $("#2").click(function() {
    $.getq('queue', '/lamp_control/digital/8/0');
  });
```

We make the same thing for the ESP8266 connected device ON:

```
//Function to control lamp ESP8266
  $("#3").click(function() {
    $.getq('queue', '/lamp_control2/digital/5/0');
  });
```

We make the same thing for the ESP8266 connected device OFF:

```
  $("#4").click(function() {
    $.getq('queue', '/lamp_control2/digital/5/1');
  });
```

Get the data from the sensors temperature and humidity:

```
function refresh_dht() {
      $.getq('queue', '/sensor/temperature', function(data) {
    $('#temperature').html("Temperature: " + data.temperature + " C");
  });

  $.getq('queue', '/sensor2/temperature2', function(data) {
      $('#temperature2').html("Temperature: " + data.temperature2 + " C");
  });

  $.getq('queue', '/sensor/humidity', function(data) {
      $('#humidity').html("Humidity: " + data.humidity + " %");
  });
          $.getq('queue', '/sensor2/humidity2', function(data) {
      $('#humidity2').html("Humidity: " + data.humidity2 + " %");
  });
});
  }
```

This code refresh the page every 10000 sec:

```
refresh_dht();
setInterval(refresh_dht, 10000);
});
```

Adding the devices to monitor and control

I can see that the system is very stable; we need to add the devices that will be monitored from the Raspberry Pi Zero with the following application in JavaScript snippet.

We create the express module and the necessary libraries:

```
var express = require('express');
var app = express();
```

We define the port that will be opened:

```
var port = 3000;
```

We configure the Jade engine for the HTML web page:

```
app.set('view engine', 'jade');
```

We make the public directory to access on it:

```
app.use(express.static(__dirname + '/public'));
```

Interface for the server instructions to be executed:

```
app.get('/', function(req, res){
res.render('interface');
});
```

We declare the arrest file with the rest request:

```
var rest = require("arest")(app);
```

This code defines the devices that will be controlled and monitored, we can add the ones that we want:

```
rest.addDevice('http','192.168.1.108');
rest.addDevice('http','192.168.1.105');
rest.addDevice('http','192.168.1.107');
rest.addDevice('http','192.168.1.110');
```

We set up the server on port 3000 and listen to the web browser clients:

```
app.listen(port);
console.log("Listening on port " + port);
```

If everything is perfectly configured, we test the application by typing the following command:

```
sudo npm install arest express jade
```

This installs the Jade platform and recognizes the aREST API from Raspberry Pi Zero.

If something is necessary to update, type the following command:

```
sudo npm install pug
```

To update the arrest express, type the following command:

```
sudo npm install pi-arest express
```

It's very important to install this package to include the arrest API:

```
sudo npm install arest --unsafe-perm
```

To run the application, go to the folder where the application is and type the following command:

```
node app.js
```

In the following screenshot, we see that the server is opening port 3000:

For the final test, we need to type the IP address of the Raspberry Pi that it has in that moment into your favorite web browser:
`http://IP_Address_of_Raspberry_Pi_Zero/port.`

In the following screenshot, we can see the control and monitor data dashboard from the Raspberry Pi Zero, published on different devices on a single web page, that's something interesting to do, such that a remote system and control panel:

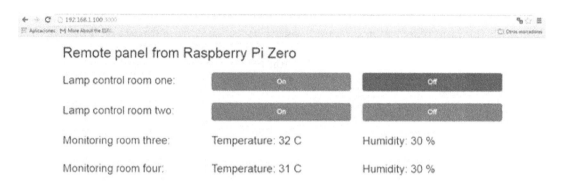

Finally, we finish by showing the control and monitor system, using different devices in a single data dashboard; we conclude that we can have more than one device in a web page for the Internet of Things.

Summary

In this chapter, you learned how to integrate and build a dashboard for monitoring and controlling using Raspberry Pi Zero with Arduino and the technologies seen in previous chapters. This chapter gave to you the basics and the necessary tools that can help you to create your own system of Internet of Things for different applications and areas that can be developed for these kinds of systems by applying all the tools, web server, database server, devices connected, and setting up your router to control your Raspberry Pi from anywhere in the world.

In the next chapter, you will build very nice devices for the Internet of Things; you will learn how to make different mini home domotics projects.

7

Building a Spy Police with the Internet of Things Dashboard

In this chapter, we will look at several home domestic projects. You can combine these projects with the other tools that we have seen in previous chapters. Doing so will help you improve your knowledge and also let you develop your own. In this chapter, the following topics will be covered:

- Spy microphone that detects noise
- Regulating the current of an AC lamp dimmer
- Controlling access with an RFID card
- Detecting smoke
- Building an alarm system using Raspberry Pi Zero
- Monitoring the climate from a remote dashboard

Spy microphone that detects noise

In this section, we will look at a project that we can use in a house to detect noise or the level of sound so that we can detect when a person talks in front of the house. This project consists of a module that has a microphone, similar to the following image:

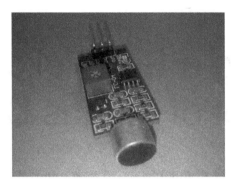

Software code

We need to make a program that can read the analog signal that the module sends to the Arduino board:

```
const int ledPin =  12;          // the number of the LED pin
const int thresholdvalue = 400; //The threshold to turn the led on

void setup() {
 pinMode(ledPin, OUTPUT);
 Serial.begin(9600);
}
void loop() {
   int sensorValue = analogRead(A0);    //use A0 to read the electrical
signal
   Serial.print("Noise detected=");
   Serial.println(sensorValue);
   delay(100);
   if(sensorValue > thresholdvalue)
   digitalWrite(ledPin,HIGH);//if the value read from A0 is larger than
400,then light the LED
   delay(200);
   digitalWrite(ledPin,LOW);
 }
```

We then download the sketch, and in the following screenshot we have the results of the level of sound:

In the following image we can see the final circuit connection to the Arduino Board:

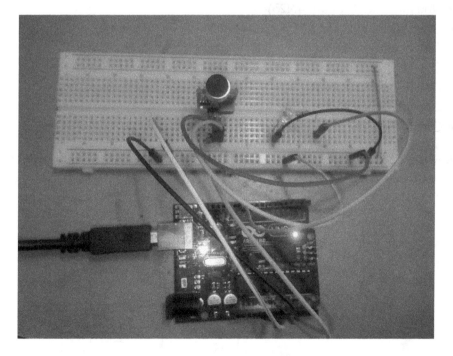

Regulating the current of an AC lamp dimmer

In this section, we will see how to regulate an AC lamp. For so many years I've wanted to explain and share a project like this, and I'm finally. This can be applied to regulate your lamps at home in order to decrease domestic power the consumption: the following sections will explain the project in more detail.

Hardware requirements

We need the following electronic components:

- H-bridge
- 24 AC transformer
- Two resistors 22k (1 watt)
- One integrated circuit (4N25)
- One resistor 10k
- One potentiometer of 5k
- One resistor 330 ohms
- One resistor 180 ohms
- One integrated circuit MOC3011
- One TRIAC 2N6073

In the following circuit diagram, we can see the connections for the dimmer from the Arduino board:

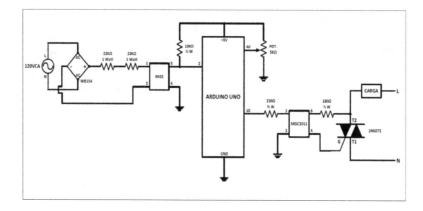

Software code

You can now either copy the code inside a file called `Dimner.ino`, or just get the complete code from the folder for this project:

```
int load = 10;
int intensity = 128;

void setup()
{
pinMode(loaf, OUTPUT);
attachInterrupt(0, cross_zero_int, RISING);
}

void loop()
{
intensity = map(analogRead(0),0,1023,10,128);
}


void cross_zero_int()
{
int dimtime = (65 * intensity);
delayMicroseconds(dimtime);
digitalWrite(load, HIGH);
delayMicroseconds(8);
digitalWrite(load, LOW);
}
```

After we have downloaded the sketch we can see the final results. With the potentiometer, we can regulate the intensity of the lamp. In our house we can have our lamps on whenever we want: maybe we can control them according the ambient light of the environment.

In the following images, we will see the different moments of lamp, if we regulate the input signal of the potentiometer:

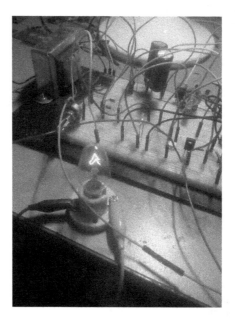

In the following image, we can see the result of regulating the brightness of the lamp:

Here we can see the dimmer of the lamp at its maximum brightness:

Controlling access with an RFID card

In this section, we will see how to control access via a door. In the last chapter, we saw how to control the lock and the lamps of a house. This project can complement the last one as it will enable you to control the opening of a door, a specific bedroom door, or lights in other rooms.

Hardware requirements

For this project, we need the following equipment:

- Reading TAGS cards
- RFID RC522 Module
- Arduino Board

The following image shows the RFID tags for reading and controlling the access:

The following figure, shows the RFID card interface for Arduino:

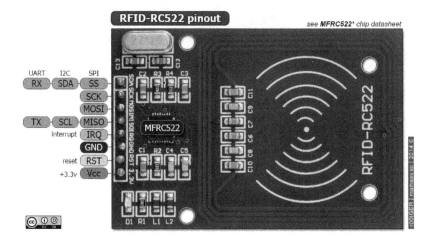

Software requirements

We need to install the `<MFRC522.h>` library, this file can communicate with and configure the module for reading the tag cards. This library can be downloaded from `https://github.com/miguelbalboa/rfid`.

Software code

You can now either copy the code inside a file called RFID.ino, or just get the complete code from the folder for this project:

```
#include <MFRC522.h>
#include <SPI.h>
#define SAD 10
#define RST 5

MFRC522 nfc(SAD, RST);

#define ledPinOpen  2
#define ledPinClose 3

void setup() {
  pinMode(ledPinOpen,OUTPUT);
  pinMode(ledPinClose,OUTPUT);

  SPI.begin();
  Serial.begin(115200);
  Serial.println("Looking for RC522");
  nfc.begin();
  byte version = nfc.getFirmwareVersion();

  if (! version) {
    Serial.print("We don't find RC522");
    while(1);
  }
  Serial.print("Found RC522");
  Serial.print("Firmware version 0x");
  Serial.print(version, HEX);
  Serial.println(".");
}

#define AUTHORIZED_COUNT 2 //number of cards Authorized
byte Authorized[AUTHORIZED_COUNT][6] = {{0xC6, 0x95, 0x39, 0x31,
0x5B},{0x2E, 0x7, 0x9A, 0xE5, 0x56}};
void printSerial(byte *serial);
boolean isSame(byte *key, byte *serial);
boolean isAuthorized(byte *serial);

void loop() {
  byte status;
  byte data[MAX_LEN];
  byte serial[5];
  boolean Open = false;
```

```
  digitalWrite(ledPinOpen, Open);
  digitalWrite(ledPinClose, !Open);
  status = nfc.requestTag(MF1_REQIDL, data);

  if (status == MI_OK) {
    status = nfc.antiCollision(data);
    memcpy(serial, data, 5);
    if(isAuthorized(serial))
    {
      Serial.println("Access Granted");
      Open = true;
    }
    else
    {
      printSerial(serial);
      Serial.println("NO Access");
      Open = false;
    }
    nfc.haltTag();
    digitalWrite(ledPinOpen, Open);
    digitalWrite(ledPinClose, !Open);
    delay(2000);
  }
  delay(500);
}

boolean isSame(byte *key, byte *serial)
{
    for (int i = 0; i < 4; i++) {
      if (key[i] != serial[i])
      {
        return false;
      }
    }
    return true;
}


boolean isAuthorized(byte *serial)
{
    for(int i = 0; i<AUTHORIZED_COUNT; i++)
    {
      if(isSame(serial, Authorized[i]))
        return true;
    }
    return false;
}
void printSerial(byte *serial)
```

```
{
    Serial.print("Serial:");
    for (int i = 0; i < 5; i++) {
    Serial.print(serial[i], HEX);
    Serial.print(" ");
    }
}
```

This is the final result when we pass the Tag card in front of the RFID module connected to the Arduino, if the code below, it will display the message (Access Granted).

In this part of the code, we configure the number of cards authorized:

```
#define AUTHORIZED_COUNT 2
byte Authorized[AUTHORIZED_COUNT][6] = {{0xC6, 0x95, 0x39, 0x31, 0x5B},
    {0x2E, 0x7, 0x9A, 0xE5, 0x56}};
```

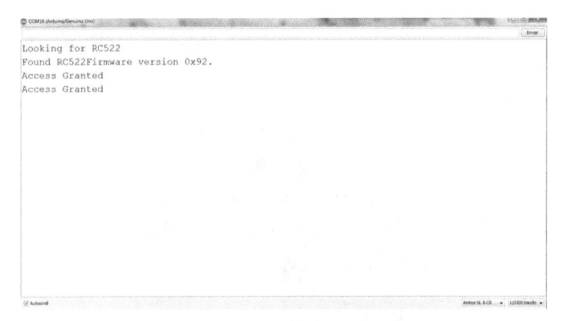

If we keep the card on the tag and card that is not registered, it can provide the correct access:

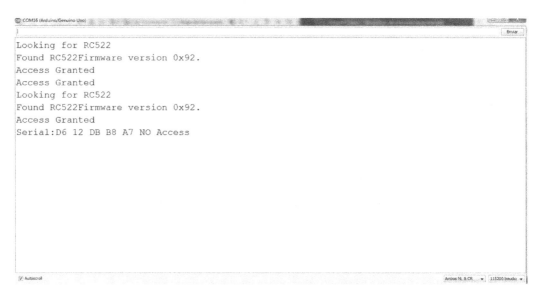

```
COM16 (Arduino/Genuino Uno)

Looking for RC522
Found RC522Firmware version 0x92.
Access Granted
Access Granted
Looking for RC522
Found RC522Firmware version 0x92.
Access Granted
Serial:D6 12 DB B8 A7 NO Access
```

The final result with the complete connections is shown in the following image:

Detecting smoke

In this section, we will test an **MQ135** sensor which can detect smoke. This could also be used in a home to detect a gas leak. In this case, we will use it to detect smoke.

In home automation systems, putting all the sensors to detect something at home, we measure the real world: in this case we used the MQ135 sensor which can detect gas and smoke, as shown in the following image:

Software code

In the following code, we explain how program and detect smoke using the gas sensor:

```
const int sensorPin= 0;
const int buzzerPin= 12;
int smoke_level;

void setup() {
Serial.begin(115200);
pinMode(sensorPin, INPUT);
pinMode(buzzerPin, OUTPUT);
}

void loop() {
smoke_level= analogRead(sensorPin);
```

```
Serial.println(smoke_level);



if(smoke_level > 200){
digitalWrite(buzzerPin, HIGH);
}

else{
digitalWrite(buzzerPin, LOW);
}
}
```

If it doesn't detect smoke, it produces the following values, as shown in the following screenshot:

If it detects smoke the measurements are in range *305* and *320* which can be seen in the file as the following screenshot:

The final result (with the complete circuit connections) is shown in the following image:

Building an alarm system using the Raspberry Pi Zero

In this section, we will build a simple alarm system with a PIR sensor connected to the Raspberry Pi Zero. This is an important project as it can be added to the home, including other sensors, in order to monitor it.

Motion sensor with Raspberry Pi Zero

For this project we need the Raspberry Pi Zero, a motion sensor PIR, and some cables. The hardware configuration for this project will actually be very simple. First, connect the **VCC** pin of the motion sensor to a **3.3V** pin on the Raspberry Pi. Then, connect the **GND** pin of the sensor to one **GND** pin on the Pi. Finally, connect the **OUT** pin of the motion sensor to the **GPIO17** pin on the Raspberry Pi. You can refer to the previous chapters to find out about pin mapping on the Raspberry Pi Zero board.

The following image shows the final circuit with the connections:

Software code

You can now either copy the code inside the folder called Project1, or just get the complete code from the folder for this project:

```
// Modules
var express = require('express');
```

```
// Express app
var app = express();

// aREST
var piREST = require('pi-arest')(app);
piREST.set_id('34f5eQ');
piREST.set_name('motion_sensor');
piREST.set_mode('bcm');

// Start server
app.listen(3000, function () {
  console.log('Raspberry Pi Zero motion sensor started!');
});
```

The alarm module

You will usually have a modules in your home that will flash a light and emit sound when motion is detected. Of course you could perfectly well connect it to a real siren instead of a buzzer to have a loud sound in case any motion is detected.

To assemble this module, first place the LED in series with the 330 Ohm resistor on the breadboard, with the longest pin of the LED in contact with the resistor. Also place the Buzzer on the breadboard. Then, connect the other side of the resistor to **GPIO14** on the Pi and the other part of the LED to one **GND** pin on the Pi. For the Buzzer, connect the pin marked + on the buzzer to **GPIO15** and the other pin on the Buzzer to one **GND** pin on the Pi.

Software code

Here we go with the coding details:

```
// Modules
var express = require('express');

// Express app
var app = express();

// aREST
var piREST = require('pi-arest')(app);
piREST.set_id('35f5fc');
piREST.set_name('alarm');
piREST.set_mode('bcm');

// Start server
```

```
app.listen(3000, function () {
  console.log('Raspberry Pi Zero alarm started!');
});
```

This is the final circuit showing the connections:

Central interface

First we create a central interface for the app using the following code:

```
// Modules
var express = require('express');
var app = express();
var request = require('request');

// Use public directory
app.use(express.static('public'));

// Pi addresses
var motionSensorPi = "192.168.1.104:3000";
var alarmPi = "192.168.1.103:3000"

// Pins
var buzzerPin = 15;
var ledPin = 14;
var motionSensorPin = 17;

// Routes
app.get('/', function (req, res) {
res.sendfile(__dirname + '/public/interface.html');
});
```

```
app.get('/alarm', function (req, res) {
  res.json({alarm: alarm});
});

app.get('/off', function (req, res) {

  // Set alarm off
  alarm = false;

  // Set LED & buzzer off
  request("http://" + alarmPi + "/digital/" + ledPin + '/0');
  request("http://" + alarmPi + "/digital/" + buzzerPin + '/0');

  // Answer
  res.json({message: "Alarm off"});

});

// Start server
var server = app.listen(3000, function() {
    console.log('Listening on port %d', server.address().port);
});

// Motion sensor measurement loop
setInterval(function() {

  // Get data from motion sensor
  request("http://" + motionSensorPi + "/digital/" + motionSensorPin,
    function (error, response, body) {

      if (!error && body.return_value == 1) {

        // Activate alarm
        alarm = true;

        // Set LED on
        request("http://" + alarmPi + "/digital/" + ledPin + '/1');


        // Set buzzer on
        request("http://" + alarmPi + "/digital/" + buzzerPin + '/1');

      }
  });

}, 2000);
```

Graphical interface

Let's now see the interface file, starting with the HTML. We start by importing all the required libraries and files for the project:

```html
<!DOCTYPE html>
<html>

<head>
  <script src="https://code.jquery.com/jquery-2.2.4.min.js"></script>
  <link rel="stylesheet"
href="https://maxcdn.bootstrapcdn.com/bootstrap/3.3.6/css/bootstrap.min.css
">
  <script
src="https://maxcdn.bootstrapcdn.com/bootstrap/3.3.6/js/bootstrap.min.js"><
/script>
  <script src="js/script.js"></script>
  <link rel="stylesheet" href="css/style.css">
  <meta name="viewport" content="width=device-width, initial-scale=1">
</head>

<script type="text/javascript">

/* Copyright (C) 2007 Richard Atterer, richardÂ©atterer.net
   This program is free software; you can redistribute it and/or modify it
   under the terms of the GNU General Public License, version 2. See the
file
   COPYING for details. */

var imageNr = 0; // Serial number of current image
var finished = new Array(); // References to img objects which have
finished downloading
var paused = false;

</script>
<div id="container">

  <h3>Security System</h3>
  <div class='row voffset50'>
  <div class='col-md-4'></div>
  <div class='col-md-4 text-center'>
      Alarm is OFF
    </div>
    <div class='col-md-4'></div>

  </div>

  <div class='row'>
```

```
    <div class='col-md-4'></div>
    <div class='col-md-4'>
      <button id='off' class='btn btn-block btn-danger'>Deactivate
Alarm</button>
    </div>
    <div class='col-md-4'></div>

  </div>

  </div>

</body>
</html>
```

Monitoring the climate from a remote dashboard

Today, most smart homes are connected to the Internet, and this allows the user to monitor their home. In this section, we are going to learn how to monitor your climate remotely. First, we are simply going to add a sensor to our Raspberry Pi Zero and monitor the measurements from a cloud dashboard. Let's see how it works.

The following image shows the final connections:

Exploring the sensor test

```
var sensorLib = require('node-dht-sensor');
var sensor = {
    initialize: function () {
        return sensorLib.initialize(11, 4);
    },
    read: function () {
        var readout = sensorLib.read();
        console.log('Temperature: ' + readout.temperature.toFixed(2) + 'C,
' +
            'humidity: ' + readout.humidity.toFixed(2) + '%');
        setTimeout(function () {
            sensor.read();
        }, 2000);
    }
};

if (sensor.initialize()) {
    sensor.read();
} else {
    console.warn('Failed to initialize sensor');
}
```

Configuring the remote dashboard (Dweet.io)

We need to go to `http://freeboard.io` and create an account:

Now, we create a new dashboard to control the sensor:

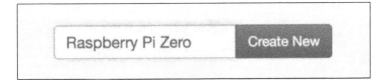

Add a new data source with the following parameters:

Create a new pane inside the dashboard and also create a **Gauge** widget for the temperature:

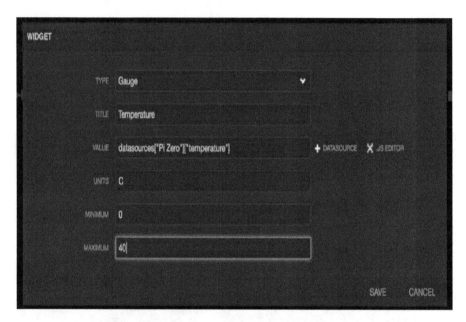

We will then immediately see the temperature in the interface:

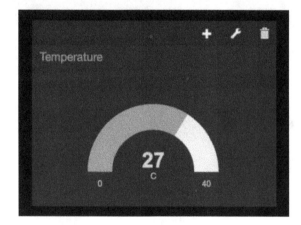

We do the same with the Humidity:

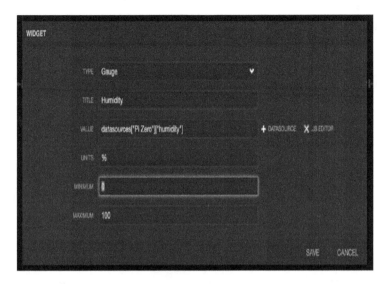

We should see the final result:

Summary

In this chapter, we learned how to build and integrate a modular security system based on Raspberry Pi Zero and Arduino boards. There are of course many ways to improve this project. For example, you can simply add more modules to the project, such as more motion sensors that trigger the same alarm. You can monitor the system, even if you are outside of the Wi-Fi network of your home.

In the next chapter, we are going to learn how to control your system from an Android application, and how to integrate a real system from your smartphone that's fantastic!

8

Monitoring and Controlling Your Devices from a Smart Phone

In previous chapters, we have seen projects that are being controlled from web interfaces. Now in this chapter, we will see how to control your Arduino and Raspberry Pi from a native application in Android, using platforms in order to create apps to control and monitor.

In this chapter, we will see different projects and applications using Android tools, the topics that will be covered are as follows:

- Controlling a relay from a smart phone using APP Inventor
- Reading JSON response in Android Studio using Ethernet shield
- Controlling a DC motor from an Android application
- Controlling outputs from Android using your Raspberry Pi Zero
- Controlling outputs with Raspberry Pi via Bluetooth

Controlling a relay from a smart phone using APP Inventor

In this section, we will see how to create an Android application using **APP Inventor** to control a relay connected to the Arduino board.

Hardware requirements

Hardware required for the project are as follows:

- Relay module
- Arduino UNO board
- Ethernet shield
- Some cables

Software requirements

Software required for the project are as follows:

- Software Arduino IDE
- You need a Gmail account activated

Creating our first application

App Inventor for Android is an open source web application originally provided by Google, and now maintained by the Massachusetts Institute of Technology (MIT). It allows newcomers to computer programming to create software applications for the Android operating system (OS). It uses a graphical interface, very similar to Scratch and the StarLogo TNG user interface, which allows users to drag-and-drop visual objects to create an application that can run on Android devices. In creating App Inventor, Google drew upon significant prior research in educational computing, as well as work done within Google on online development environments.

You don't need to install any software for APP inventor to execute in your computer; you just need your Gmail account to access the APP inventor interface.

To enter APP Inventor you just need to go to: `http://appinventor.mit.edu/explore/`.

Go to create apps to start designing the app.

First we need to have an account with Gmail; we need to create the file like we see in the following screenshot:

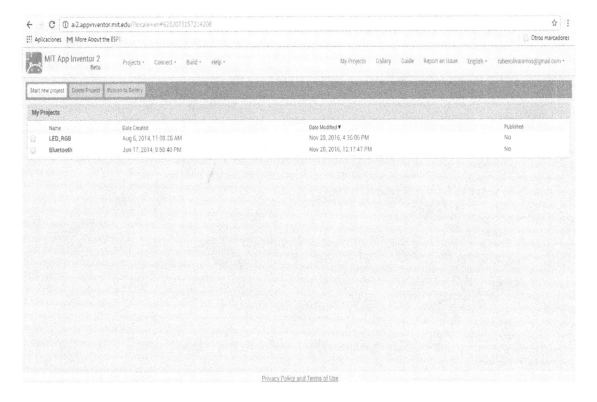

Go to menu **Projects** and **Start New Project**:

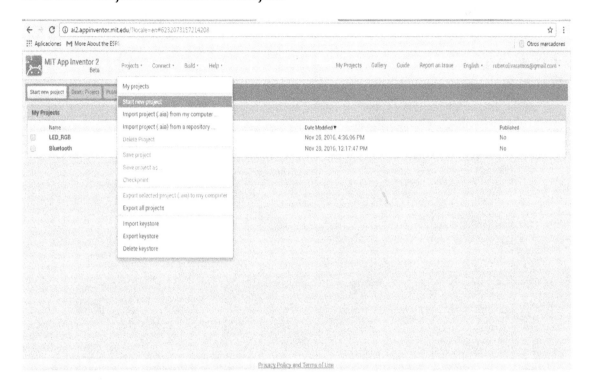

Write the name of the project:

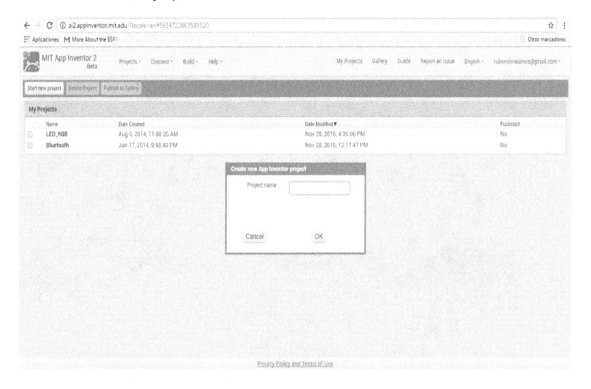

In the following screenshot, we write the name of our project as **aREST**:

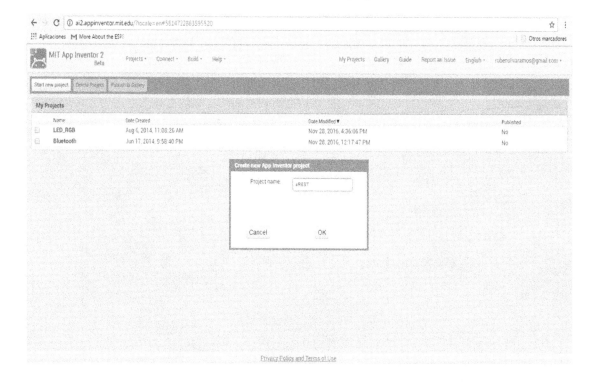

On pressing **OK**, we will see the project created:

Designing the interface

Now it's time to see how to create the interface of the application, after we create the project we click on the name of the project, and we will then see the following screen:

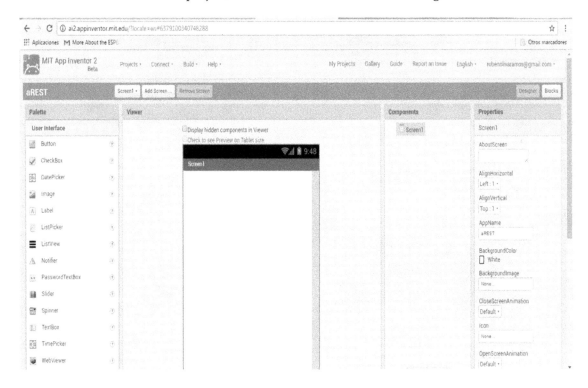

In the user interface that we have on the left-hand side (you can see all the objects), to move an object to the main screen you just drag **Web Viewer** and **Button**, as shown in the following screenshot:

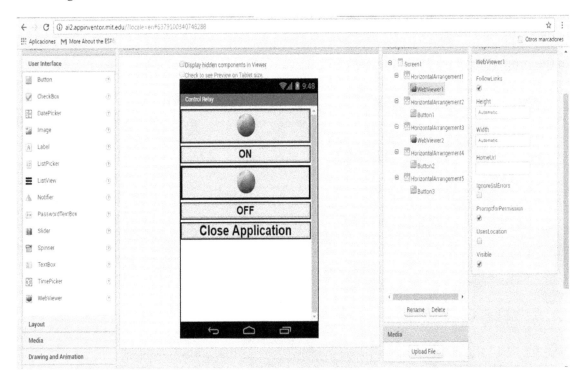

In the previous screenshot, we can see the interface of the app that we will use to control our Arduino board.

Communicating APP Inventor with Arduino ethernet shield

Now we will see how to communicate the application with Arduino via Ethernet networking.

In the properties of the **Web Viewer** control, we will see the home URL:

In both controls we have the URL of our Arduino Ethernet shield, we will make a request using the RESTful services, and we will send the following requests from the application:

- http://192.168.1.110/digital/7/1
- http://192.168.1.110/digital/7/0

Code for APP Inventor

The blocks editor in the original version ran in a separate Java process, using the `Open Blocks Java` library for creating visual blocks programming languages and programming.

We have the code for APP inventor, when we click the buttons we call the web service, to do that you just need to do the following:

- Go to the screen interface that says **Blocks**
- Drag the `When...Do` block one per button
- Inside the block that you just dragged before, put the `Call...WebViewer.GoToUrl` block
- In the URL of the block, put the `WebViewer.HomeUrl` block

To close the application:

- Drag the `When...Button.Click Do` block
- And inside the block put the close application block

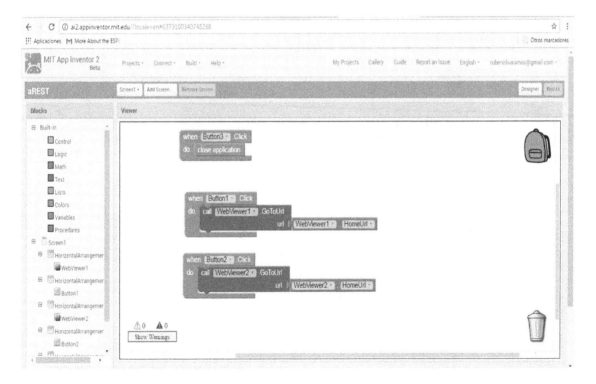

We will have the following results when we open a web browser:

{"message": "Pin D7 set to 0", "id": "1", "name": "APPInventor", "connected": true}

The following screenshot shows the application running on a mobile phone:

The following image shows the final results with the connections:

Reading JSON response in Android Studio using ethernet shield

In this section, we will see how to read responses reading from the Arduino board and reading in Android Studio.

Before we continue with the next part, we need to do the following:

- Instal the IDE of Android Studio,which can be obtained from: `https://develope r.android.com/studio/index.html?hl=es-419`
- Get the latest SDK for Android Studio

Then we will create a project in Android Studio, as shown in the following screenshot:

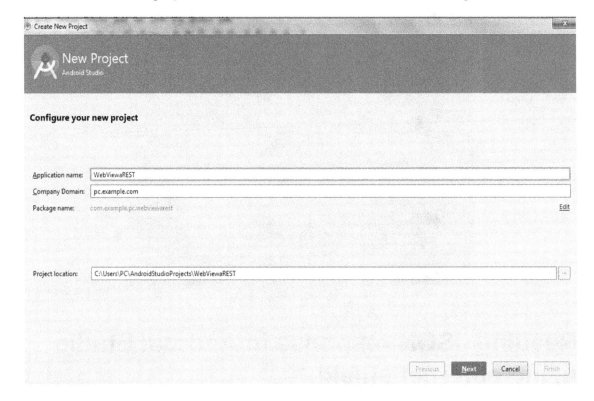

We then select the version of the API that we want to use and click the **Next** button:

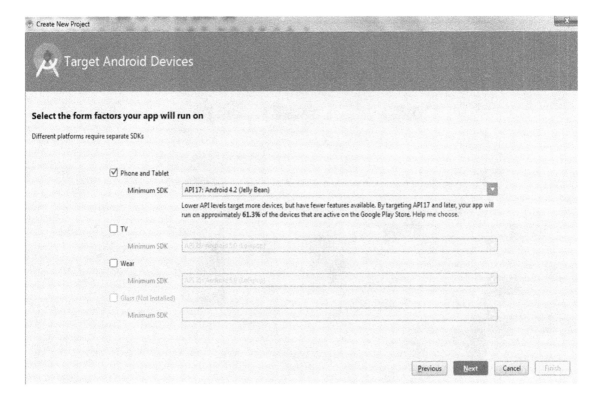

Then select a **Blank Activity** and click on the **Next** button:

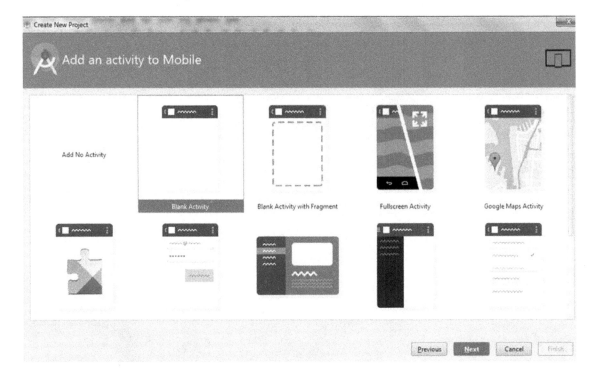

Type the name of your Activity and the Layout, and then click the **Finish** button:

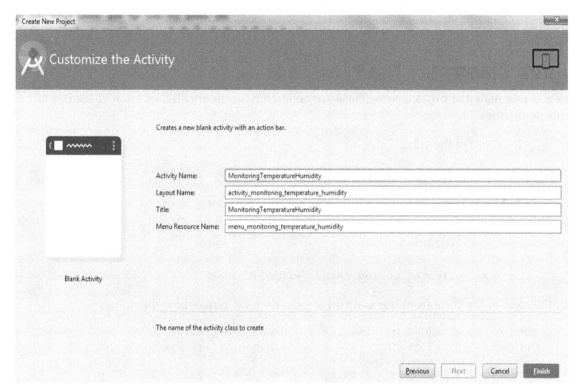

Android application

In this section, we will see the android application. In your folder, open the file of the project about Android Studio.

We have here the XML code generated in the code of the interface:

```
FrameLayout xmlns:android="http://schemas.android.com/apk/res/android"
    xmlns:tools="http://schemas.android.com/tools"
    android:id="@+id/container"
    android:layout_width="match_parent"
    android:layout_height="match_parent"
    tools:context=".MainActivity">
    tools:ignore="MergeRootFrame">

    <WebView
        android:id="@+id/activity_main_webview"
```

```
            android:layout_width="match_parent"
            android:layout_height="match_parent" />
    </FrameLayout>
```

Java class

When we create the project, some class are generated automatically, as we will see in the following lines:

1. Name of the class:

   ```
   import android.webkit.WebView;
   ```

2. Main class:

   ```
   public class MonitoringTemperatureHumidity extends
       ActionBarActivity {

           private WebView mWebView;
   ```

In this part of the code from the android application, we request for the value:

```
mWebView.loadUrl("http://192.168.1.110/temperature");
mWebView.loadUrl("http://192.168.1.110/humidity");
super.onCreate(savedInstanceState);
setContentView(R.layout.activity_monitoring_temperature_humidity);
```

We define the objects that will be included in the main activity, in this case it is the `mWebView` control, it is defined in the main activity of the application:

```
    mWebView = (WebView)  findViewById(R.id.activity_main_webview);
    mWebView.loadUrl("http://192.168.1.110/humidity");
}
```

Permission of the application

In order to give permission to the application to execute networking permissions, it's necessary that we add the following line in the Android Manifest file:

```
<uses-permission android:name="android.permission.INTERNET"/>
```

When the application is debugged and installed on the device, we will see the following results on our screen, displaying the value of the `temperature`:

The value of the `humidity`:

Controlling a DC motor using an Android Application

In this section, we will have an application to link our smart phone with the Bluetooth of the phone, it's called **Amarino** and you can get it from: `http://www.amarino-toolkit.net/index.php/home.html`. We will also see how to control a DC motor from an Android application, let's dive into it!

Hardware requirements

In the following diagram, we see the following circuit (L293D) is used to control the speed and the turning of the motor:

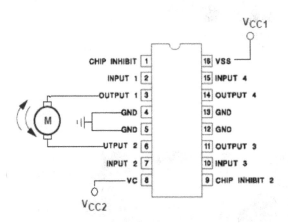

In the following figure, we have the final connections of the circuit to the Arduino board:

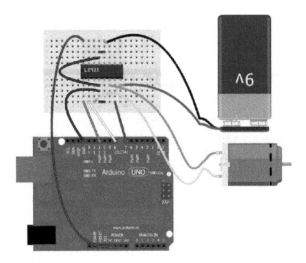

The final interface is shown in the following screenshot:

The final results are shown in the following image with the connections:

Controlling outputs from android using your Raspberry Pi Zero

In this section, we will see how to control our outputs connected to the Raspberry Pi, using the `control.js` script running in the `Node.js` server.

The request that we need to control over the LED output using the android application are as follows:

1. `http://192.168.1.111:8099/ledon`
2. `http://192.168.1.111:8099/ledoff`

The interface created in APP Inventor will be similar to the following screenshot:

The final circuit connections would look like the following screenshot:

Controlling outputs with Raspberry Pi via Bluetooth

Things go a different route as soon as you're trying to communicate with other electronic gadgets that uses Bluetooth modules connected to the serial port of the Raspberry Pi.

These modules are very cheap to buy, the actual module is the green board that sits on the breakout board in my model. The pure HC-05 will only work on *3.3V* levels, not with *5V-TTL*-levels. So one would need level shifters (again).

In this section, we will communicate the Raspberry Pi Zero to the Bluetooth module, and connect the pins **TX** and **RX** of the Raspberry Pi.

First, we need to configure the file of the system to make some changes in order to activate the communication of the Raspberry Pi Zero TX and RX:

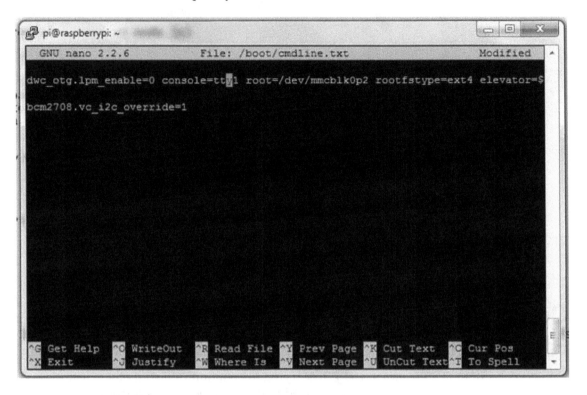

Controlling lights from an Android Application

We need to download the Bluetooth Terminal, as shown in the following screenshot:

The following screenshot shows the results of sending the numbers 1, 2, 3, 4, 5, and 6:

```
pi@raspberrypi: ~
the exact distribution terms for each program are described in the
individual files in /usr/share/doc/*/copyright.

Debian GNU/Linux comes with ABSOLUTELY NO WARRANTY, to the extent
permitted by applicable law.
Last login: Mon Dec  5 20:04:53 2016
pi@raspberrypi:~ $ sudo python ch06_01.py
initializing...
opening serial port
True
running now
RCV: 1
RCV: 2
RCV: 3
RCV: 4
RCV: 5
RCV: 6
RCV: 1
RCV: 2
RCV: 3
RCV: 4
RCV: 5
RCV: 6
```

The following image shows the final part of the project and the connections with the HC05 module and the Raspberry Pi Zero:

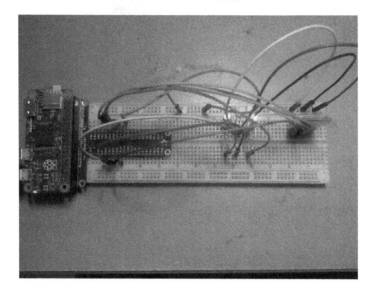

Summary

In this chapter, you learned how to control your Arduino and Raspberry Pi Zero from a smartphone using Android Studio and APP inventor, via Bluetooth and Ethernet communication. We also looked at several projects such as controlling a motor, controlling a relay module, and reading humidity and temperature. For future projects you can now control and monitor anything you want in any area of the application you want.

In the next chapter, we will integrate everything from the previous chapters and put it all together to integrate all the knowledge applying all the things.

9
Putting It All Together

The previous chapters have provided us with the foundation and elements to design and put together our entire domestic system, which we will study in this chapter. I hope that I've guided you through this journey in a fairly structured and logical way, so that you are ready to do that.

As a guide to building the whole system, in this chapter, we will guide you through how to integrate and give you some ideas to put everything together, and also give you the final details. You can then make your own projects with the ideas that we will mention in this final chapter.

In this chapter, we will cover the following topics:

- Integrating the system – development projects
- Controlling access with a matrix keyboard
- Integrating the system control with relays and devices
- How to set up the power supplies

Integrating the system – development projects

In the previous chapters, we have seen different projects on home automation and domestic that is control and monitor home appliances. In this chapter, we will give some ideas to develop some projects that they can be done in different areas using electronics, controlling and monitoring.

Getting into the details of light sensor

As its name implies, the **Light Dependent Resistor (LDR)** is made from a piece of exposed semiconductor material, such as cadmium sulfide, that changes its electrical resistance from several thousand Ohms in the dark to only a few hundred Ohms when light falls upon it, by creating hole-electron pairs in the material. The net effect is an improvement in its conductivity, with a decrease in resistance for an increase in illumination. Also, photosensitive cells have a long response, time requiring many seconds to respond to a change in the light intensity.

In this section, we will look at how to use a light sensor to control different devices:

- On/off lights when needed
- Dimming the lamp when the sensor detects if there is light in the room or not

You can dim the lamp with the signal sensor; according to the measurement taken by the light sensor you can regulate the intensity of it.

Motion sensor

A motion sensor detects body heat (infrared energy). Passive infrared sensors are the most widely used motion in home security systems. When your system is armed, your motion sensors are activated. Once the sensor warms up, it can detect heat and movement in the surrounding areas, creating a protective grid.

If a moving object blocks too many grid zones and the infrared energy levels change rapidly, the sensors are tripped. Using this sensor we can control lights when we want them turn on or turn off:

According to the distance the sensor measures, it can detect the object so you can control the lamp:

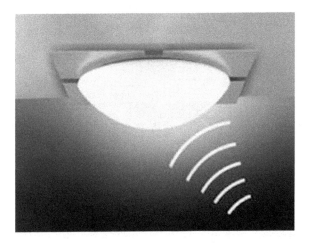

Automatic light controller

Sensors work when you are not home, or when you tell the system you are not there. Some security systems can be programmed to record events via a security camera when motion is detected. The main purpose of motion detection is to sense an intruder and send an alert to your control panel, which alerts your monitoring center:

The following circuit diagram show the connection for an automatic light control where we use all the elements used earlier like the LDR sensor, PIR sensor, and the relay module:

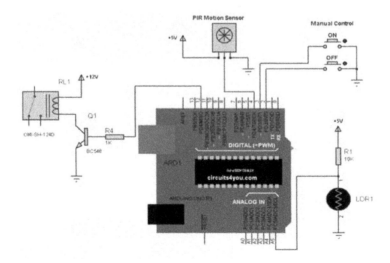

Solar power monitor circuit

Here we have another real project that shows a control panel that will monitor the energy of the solar panel using the Arduino board. The following diagram shows the connection of the sensors and solar panel to Arduino board:

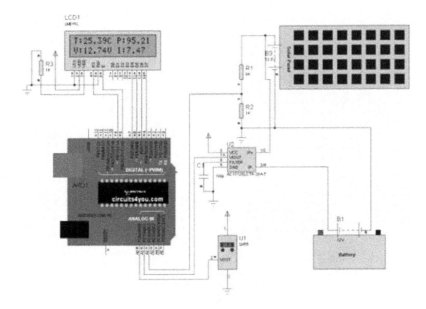

Automatic irrigation system with a soil sensor

In the following figure, we have another project; we are integrating the tools that were used before. In this case, we will control the watering when it is present or not, using a soil sensor:

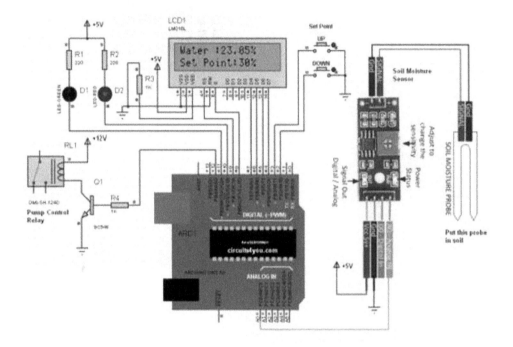

Until now you have seen very interesting and valuable projects that can be applied to real situations, in different areas, such as domestic, home automation, and even in a garden. In the following sections we will look at more projects. Let's do it!

Arduino water-level controller

In this project, we will make an automatic level sensor to control the level of water using your Arduino board, as shown in the following diagram:

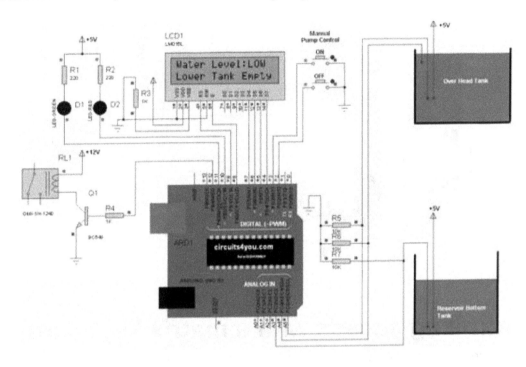

Bluetooth based home automation

In this section, we will look at a project that can be used in home automation, to control the devices in a house, using a Bluetooth module to communicate, and a relay module and the integration of the hardware as software tools.

The following diagram shows how to connect the relay module and the HC05 Bluetooth module to the Arduino board:

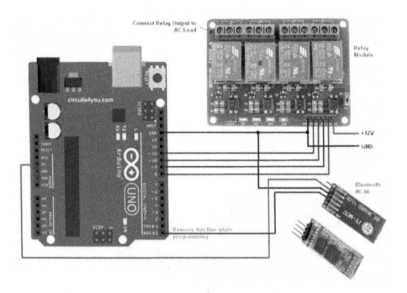

Controlling access with a matrix keyboard

In this section, we will look at how to control the access with a code using a matrix keyboard. In the following image, we can see the keyboard that we will use:

The keypad

In the following diagram, we see the hardware connections to the Arduino board. They are connected to the digital pins:

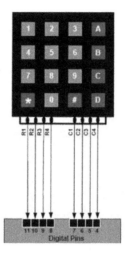

Connecting an LCD screen to display the code

In the following diagram, we show the hardware connections of the LCD screen to the Arduino board:

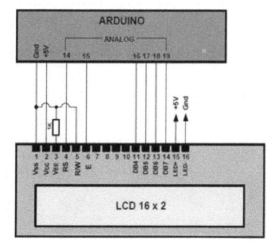

We have looked at some interesting projects that you can develop by adding new sensor to control other devices. In the next section, we will look at a very interesting project. Get ready for the next step, this is a great goal.

Controlling the door lock with a keypad

In the following image, we see a keypad with a lock. This section can be merged along with the last project. This device can be controlled from your Raspberry Pi Zero or your Arduino board:

Code to access using the keypad

You can now either copy the code inside a file called Project_keyboard_Access_Control.ino, or just get the complete code from the folder for this project using the Arduino IDE:

```
void captura()
{
  tecla = customKeypad.getKey();

  if (tecla)
  {
    digito = digito + 1;
if(tecla==35){tecla=0;digito=0;valorf=0;lcd.setCursor(0,0);lcd.print(valorf
);
```

```
            lcd.print ("                    ");}
        if(tecla==48){tecla=0;}
        if(tecla==42){tecla=0;digito=0;valor = valorf;}

     if(digito==1){valorf1 = tecla; valorf=valorf1;lcd.setCursor(0,0);
            lcd.print(valorf);lcd.print("                ");}
       if(digito==2){valorf2 =
tecla+(valorf1*10);valorf=valorf2;lcd.setCursor(0,0);
            lcd.print(valorf);lcd.print("                ");}
       if(digito==3){valorf3 =
tecla+(valorf2*10);valorf=valorf3;lcd.setCursor(0,0);
            lcd.print(valorf);lcd.print("                ");}
       if(digito==4){valorf4 =
tecla+(valorf3*10);valorf=valorf4;lcd.setCursor(0,0);
            lcd.print(valorf);lcd.print("                ");}
       if(digito==5){valorf5 =
tecla+(valorf4*10);valorf=valorf5;lcd.setCursor(0,0);
            lcd.print(valorf);lcd.print("                ");digito=0;}
     }
```

This function checks if the code that was typed is correct:

```
void loop()
{
  captura();
  if (valor == 92828)
  {
    digitalWrite(lock,HIGH);
  }
  if (valor == 98372)
  {
    digitalWrite(lock,LOW);
  }
}
```

Integrating the system control with relays and devices

In the following figure, we're integrating important parts of the book. We will show the connections in a house using a relay, and how you will apply and control the real load using a lamp:

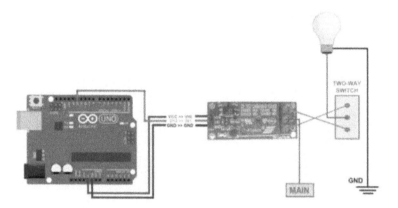

Controlling multiple appliances

In real life, we will see the devices connected and controlling the real world. In the following image, we can see the relay module that can control the loads with the electronics part:

The following image shows the final circuit. We see the real connections to the Arduino board, and how they control the real world.

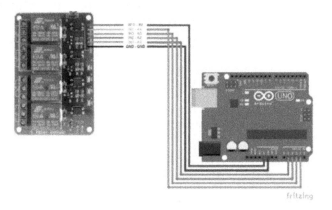

The complete system

In the following figure, we see the final circuit for controlling real devices in a home automation system. This can be used in all areas of the home, in each room we can have a relay module, connected to each module communicating with control system:

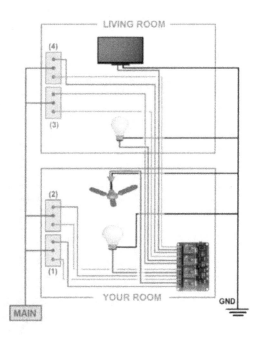

How to set up the power supplies

For our system, it is very important to set up the power supply that will be used in the system. First we need to ensure that the voltage for the Arduino is about *5V*. In the following diagram, we have shown how to configure the voltage to about 5 volts:

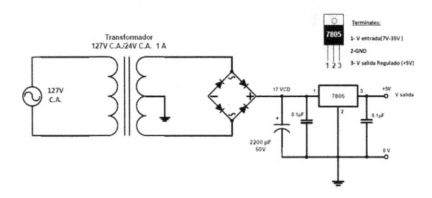

Power supply for AC loads

If we need to connect AC loads to the Arduino or Raspberry Pi Zero and make an industrial control system, we need to use a voltage of 24 V of DC, as you can see in the following circuit diagram:

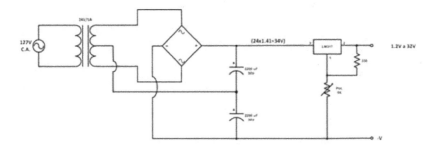

Connecting a relay of 24 DC volts to the Arduino board

In the following diagram, we have the circuit to control an AC load using a relay of 24 volts of DC:

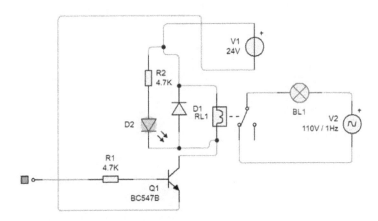

We have the final circuit, which represents the interface to control an AC load, connected to the output digital pin to the Raspberry Pi Zero or the Arduino board: this is not very common to see, but it's necessary to learn how to connect a relay that can be energized with 24 volts of DC to the Arduino board:

Finally we have the final circuit in a board. We used a relay that has a coil, which has to energize with 24 volts. The digital output of the Arduino or Raspberry Pi can be connected to the relay module.

Summary

This is the last chapter of the book, *Internet of Things Programming with JavaScript*. In this chapter, you learned how to integrate all the elements that you need to take into consideration when you want to apply the tools of hardware and software in the projects that we showed you. This is going to help you to continue developing your own projects, following the basics and the knowledge shared in this book.

Index

www.ingramcontent.com/pod-product-compliance
Lightning Source LLC
Chambersburg PA
CBHW060517060326
40690CB00017B/3311